Praise for *The Leadership Baton*

No vision for leadership development proves to be more holistic and effective than church-based training. While many have seen the need for anchoring the training of future chu____ ____ders in the church, no one I know has been as dedicated to find____ ____ ____ ____ as this capable team of Forman, Jones, and Miller. _____ work but one that *has* worked in the var_____. The church worldwide will be stronge _____ ciples of *The Leadership Baton*.

RANDY FRAZEE, ____
of *The Connecting Church*
and *Making Room for Life*

What a thrill to read this book! It has been written by men who have served alongside me—and each other—in developing what we believe is a biblical and practical strategy for developing leaders in the local church. What they write is not just theory; they are practitioners. Though at various stages along the way I have been their mentor, all three authors have served as key leaders in my own life.

GENE A. GETZ, pastor emeritus,
Fellowship Bible Church North,
Plano, Texas

Three "church-wise" practitioners place the emphasis for leadership development precisely where it belongs—on the local church! A highly practical, biblically sound approach to what we must be about—the training of church leaders.

AUBREY MALPHURS, author
of *Being Leaders*
and *Church Next*

The Leadership Baton is a manual on developing godly church leaders written by three men who are committed to the spiritual health of the local church. Forman, Jones, and Miller are not "armchair" leaders. Their lives intersect with church life at every turn. This book reflects their passion to help every church leader impact followers by using biblical principles.

ELIZABETH INRIG, national director
of women's ministries,
Evangelical Free Church of America

In one volume the authors have identified and responded to a myriad of leadership training issues. The result is a highly practical and comprehensive blueprint for leadership development in the local church. Inspirational and challenging reading!

BRIAN KEANE, senior pastor,
Edwardstown Baptist Church,
Adelaide, South Australia

In recent decades we've witnessed the rediscovery of church-based evangelism, community, and spirituality. Now, thanks to resources like *The Leadership Baton*, church-based leadership development is no longer an idle dream—it is becoming an emerging reality.

BILL DONAHUE, author
of *Leading Life-Changing
Small Groups*

The Leadership Baton pioneers the much-needed integration of character development, academic studies, and grassroots experience in the formation of leaders for our churches. This is a very practical, helpful book, authored by people who have effectively worked out in their own experience everything they've written about.

JIM PETERSEN, author
of *Living Proof* and
Church Without Walls

After interacting with the authors for over a decade, I know firsthand their praiseworthy passion, portable principles, and persistent practice related to developing leadership in the local church. Apply the teaching of this book, and you will ensure the maturing of your local church and the expansion of Christ's kingdom on earth throughout the next generation.

LEROY R. ARMSTRONG, JR., senior pastor,
St. John Missionary Baptist Church,
Dallas, Texas

This new movement known as church-based training promises to return Christian ministry to biblical patterns of leadership development. *The Leadership Baton* shows how to develop leaders within the church for ministry in the twenty-first century.

KERBY ANDERSON, president,
Probe Ministries

ROWLAND FORMAN
JEFF JONES
BRUCE MILLER

The LEADERSHIP BATON

AN INTENTIONAL STRATEGY FOR DEVELOPING LEADERS IN YOUR CHURCH

ZONDERVAN®

ZONDERVAN.com/
AUTHORTRACKER
follow your favorite authors

The Leadership Baton
Copyright © 2004 by Rowland Forman, Jeff Jones, and Bruce Miller

Requests for information should be addressed to:

Zondervan, *Grand Rapids, Michigan 49530*

Library of Congress Cataloging-in-Publication Data

Forman, Rowland, 1943-
    The leadership baton : an intentional strategy for developing leaders in your church /
Rowland Forman, Jeff Jones, and Bruce Miller.
       p. cm.
    Includes bibliographical references and index.
    ISBN-10: 0-310-28480-5
    ISBN-13: 978-0-310-28480-2
    1. Christian leadership. 2. Leadership—Religious aspects—Christianity.
I. Jones, Jeff, 1966- II. Miller, Bruce, 1961- III. Title
BV652.1 .F63 2004
253—dc22
                                    2003024442

Interior design by Beth Shagene

Printed in the United States of America

08 09 10 11 12 13 • 10 9 8 7 6 5 4 3 2

To Gene Getz,
who has inspired us and encouraged us
to put these ideas into practice and then into writing.
Gene serves as an amazing model
of godly leadership
for Christ's church.
His teachable spirit, genuine faith, and compassionate love
compel our loyalty and respect.
Gene is the real thing in private as well as in public.

"The things you have heard me say in the presence of many witnesses entrust to reliable men who will also be qualified to teach others."

2 Timothy 2:2 NIV

"You have heard me teach many things that have been confirmed by many reliable witnesses. Teach these great truths to trustworthy people who are able to pass them on to others."

2 Timothy 2:2 NLT

"Pass on what you heard from me—the whole congregation saying Amen!—to reliable leaders who are competent to teach others."

2 Timothy 2:2 The Message

"You should teach people whom you can trust the things you and many others have heard me say. Then they will be able to teach others."

2 Timothy 2:2 NCV

CONTENTS

FOREWORD

What you are about to read will change the way you think. Too often we perceive leadership as one-dimensional with a single-generation mind-set. *The Leadership Baton* undertakes one of the most important works of our era: It will help you to think trans-generationally about mentoring fresh, emerging leaders.

Someone once said, "Races are won or lost in the passing of the baton." I agree, but allow me to make one correction. Although passing a baton can take just a moment, it's the *heart* behind the passing of this baton that may take decades.

This is where races will be won or lost.

We can no longer hastily pass mutated batons. In fact, the whole message of the Old Testament is about successfully passing the heart of faith from one generation to another. And we can only succeed in this if we learn the lessons *before* the pass, not after it. When Jesus arrived on the scene, it was not the succession that was missing; it was the heart and the spirit behind it.

The Leadership Baton offers key insights that will build a dependable tarmac for future leaders. It resonates with my own heart and what we are doing in the South Pacific. It is not only a timely treatise but also a current word to today's churches. I often wonder what King Saul's legacy would have been if he had only mentored that young shepherd boy David rather than become intimidated by him. Then, instead of his tragic end, he could have been known as one of the greatest disciplers and tutors of all time!

Forman, Jones, and Miller are practitioners who speak not from theory but from scars, from victories, and, yes, even from defeats. This book combines voices of experience, narrating in real time the discovering and developing of emerging leaders.

The Leadership Baton is the missing link of leadership succession, a practical approach to planting our future so all who come behind us will have found us faithful!

WAYNE CORDEIRO, senior pastor,
New Hope Christian Fellowship,
Honolulu, Hawaii

ACKNOWLEDGMENTS

A Team Effort

We acknowledge the faithful staff at the Center for Church Based Training. Many of the ideas in the book were tested and improved through the efforts of CCBT as they interacted with hundreds of churches. Specifically we recognize James Roberts, the president of CCBT, whose constant encouragement has helped make this book a reality. We are also indebted to Eddy Hall for his work as an "editorial doctor." It has been a joy to work with the Zondervan team—Paul Engle, Dirk Buursma, Alicia Mey, Jamie Hinojosa, Rob Monacelli, and Beth Shagene.

Rowland Forman

If it's true that life is all about passing the baton of God's truth and grace to successive generations, then I must acknowledge my godly grandmother Bella Miller. When I was a young boy, she made Bible characters come alive and constantly expressed her belief in me. I want to acknowledge my wife of thirty-five fulfilling years—Elaine. Together we have transferred the same baton to our three incredible children, Rochelle, Mark, and David, and are more recently handing it off to our four magnificent grandsons.

I'm so grateful for the "relay team" that has taught me all I know about mentorship: Rick Murphy, Steve Burgason, Campbell Forlong, Steve Thurman, Alan McPherson, Harry Manihera, Don Overton, Mark Boyd, Jonathan Dove, Brad Carr, Robert Murchison, and Norm Hitzges. We laughed, learned, and ran farther because God made our paths cross.

My special thanks to the CCBT "dream team" I'm privileged to run the race with: James Roberts, Calvin Knox, Lisa Marcheschi, Steve Crow, Shannon Hanson, and Page Borski.

Jeff Jones

First, to my wonderful wife, Christy, thank you for your untiring love, encouragement, and support. I love you. To my two boys, Collin and Caleb, thank you, too, for being 100 percent whom God created you to be. I can't wait to see how God continues to develop you to serve him your whole lives. A million thanks are also due my parents for their unswerving belief in me.

To my church family, Fellowship Bible Church North, Plano, Texas, a profound expression of thanks is due. This book is a compilation of learnings from many different people. God used Fellowship to "re-illusion" me with the local church and to develop me in the context of ministry. I must also acknowledge our elders and pastors who have modeled the principles in this book, especially my team members at Fellowship who have encouraged me and shaped my life: Kenton Getz, Mike Hogan, Steve McPherson, Don Overton, and Jack Warren. What a thrill to serve with all of you. Our adult ministries pastor Glen Brechner has also done an extraordinary job experimenting with and implementing many of the principles in this book.

In helping with my part of the writing, my superhero/assistant Barb Alderson was extremely helpful, as was Felix Heimberg.

Bruce Miller

I thank my church family at McKinney Fellowship Bible Church, McKinney, Texas, for the privilege of serving as their pastor. Thank you for putting up with my weaknesses and my flawed attempts to lead us forward in developing leaders for Christ's church. That this book exists is a tribute to you, your prayers for me, and your love for me. Specifically, I thank our elders—Dick Best, Dave Bugno, Don Closson, Dave Lewis, and Ron Ryan—who watch over me and my family with Christlike care. It is a joy to grow together and to serve Christ together.

To my mom and dad, deepest thanks for believing in me and praying for me my whole life. I also thank my five children—Bart, Jimmy, David, Melanie, and Ben—for graciously not complaining when Dad needed to once again take time for "the book." Most of all, no human being deserves more of my gratitude than my precious wife, Tamara. Thank you, Tamara, for all that you are to me.

PREFACE:
THE STORY BEHIND
THIS BOOK

Jeff: It all started in that long, narrow classroom, 7:30 in the morning, with a young, bearded professor (Bruce), Rowland, and me sitting next to each other. None of the three of us at that point could have dreamed that one day God would bond our hearts, minds, and ministries together.

Bruce: It was my first semester as a professor at Dallas Theological Seminary (DTS). Before my first class, I got on my knees in my office and prayed to God because I was scared to death. In my Prolegomena (Introduction to Theology) class was a young seminarian, Jeff Jones, who was preparing for a career as a pastor. In the same class was Rowland Forman, a veteran pastor, teacher, and Bible college principal from New Zealand, who was working on a Doctor of Ministry (D.Min.) degree at Denver Seminary and two masters degrees at DTS with the goal of returning to New Zealand to start a seminary.

Rowland: In preparation for starting a seminary, I interviewed ten of my favorite professors, asking them the same question: "If you were starting a seminary from scratch, how would you go about it?" To my surprise, nine out of ten told me they would start a seminary that emphasized on-the-job training, much like the way airline pilots and surgeons are trained.

Bruce: I was focused on a career as an academician. At twenty-eight years old, I dreamed of spending the next forty years of my life training a generation of church leaders through the seminary.

Rowland: I had a growing desire to offer training in the local church comparable to what students were getting at the Bible college where I had served. How could we move the local church from the back end of the training process to the front end? When I shared my longings with Bruce and asked him what it would look like if he were to start a seminary from scratch, he told me, "There's no need to reinvent the wheel. Church-based training is already happening." In fact, Bruce invited me and my wife, Elaine, to join a church-based training class on Acts that he was leading for the elders and their wives at Fellowship Bible Church North, Plano, Texas. I learned more in that class than I learned in many of my seminary courses.

Bruce: I became aware of church-based training in 1989 when our pastor, Dr. Gene Getz, introduced me to Jeff Reed of the Biblical Institute of Leadership Development (BILD) in Ames, Iowa, a pioneer organization dedicated to church-based training. Instantly I could see how church-based training combined my two passions—my love for academics and my love for the local church—through its mission of training leaders in, by, and for churches. Dr. Getz asked me to implement a church-based training program at Fellowship. Jeff, who was a youth ministry intern there at the time, also became my intern, working with me to develop Fellowship's church-based training program.

Jeff: I was a seminary student at the same time we were starting the church-based training initiative. In seminary I gained more knowledge. In church-based training I saw people developing more wisdom.

Rowland: In seminary the professor's job was to bring students up to his or her level. With church-based training, where meetings took place in homes, everyone came prepared and we learned from each other.

Bruce: Church-based training was also more directly missional because we were a group of people from the same church exploring how to reach our community for Jesus Christ.

Jeff: What united the three of us was our passion to see leaders raised up and equipped through the local church. Not only were Bruce and I working together at Fellowship, but we were deeply involved in the work of BILD, often visiting Ames, Iowa, and working to extend church-based training through regional workshops.

Rowland: When I went back to New Zealand, I wanted to contextualize the concepts I had learned through church-based training. I'd been an educator since my high school teaching days, so I began writing courses and started Church-Based Training (New Zealand; on the Web at www.cbtnz.com).

Bruce: Eventually we focused on founding our own organization to further church-based training. We thanked God for what we had learned from the pioneer ministry of BILD, and the three of us—along with Willi Giefing who had founded a church-based ministry in Austria[1]—established an informal network, which led in 1995 to the founding of the Center for Church Based Training (CCBT; on the Web at www.ccbt.org). CCBT writes and publishes church-based training resources, conducts conferences and regional workshops, and provides consulting. Since 1995 CCBT has distributed over thirty thousand courses to over a thousand churches, and courses have been translated into six languages. This book is an outgrowth of the ministry God has given us since we began this process fifteen years ago.

About the Authors

Rowland Forman is a former pastor, the founder of Church-Based Training (New Zealand), and director of curriculum development for the Center for Church Based Training.

Jeff Jones is senior pastor of Fellowship Bible Church North in Plano, Texas, and executive director of the Center for Church Based Training.

Bruce Miller is senior pastor of McKinney Fellowship Bible Church in McKinney, Texas, which he founded in 1997. He also chairs the board of the Center for Church Based Training.

INTRODUCTION:
THE BATON
IN YOUR HAND

Picture yourself in a race—not just any race, but a relay race. To win, you know you need to run well, and you do. You are off and running with all you've got. People in the stands are cheering. As you approach the end of your leg, you feel both adrenaline and pride coursing through your veins. Coming around the last corner, you see the next runner. He is poised, hand in position, ready to receive the baton. You have run well, but your part is not over. You have a baton to pass. To win the race, you must hand off the baton—and you must do it well.

Now let's come back to reality. If you are a leader in a local church, you are in a relay race. Nearly two thousand years ago Jesus handed the baton to his disciples. He gave to them the mission of the church, and they ran a good race. Just as important as running a good race was passing the baton to others. As Timothy, for example, received the baton from Paul, he understood that his job was to look for others to whom he would pass the baton.

Over the centuries this baton has been passed down from Jesus, to the disciples, to others, and to others still. At some point, a leader believed in you enough to hand you the baton of leadership. Now you hold that baton. The mission of God, the mission of the local church, is in your grasp. Can you see in your imagination the baton right in front of you now? If you can, notice the fingerprints on it— the fingerprints of those who passed the baton to you, as well as those who passed it to them. And beneath all those fingerprints, the fingerprints of Jesus. Now it is your turn to pass the baton to other emerging leaders who will continue the race.

Christianity is always just one generation away from extinction. So it is for your church and mine. It has always been this way. Jesus' mission has always depended on one generation of leaders handing the mission to the next. Where they have done so effectively, their churches and ministries have continued to thrive. Now the mission is in your grasp.

Just what is this mission that has been handed to us? In order to faithfully run the race and pass on the mission, we must be clear about what it is. In Matthew 16:18 Jesus told us what he would be doing on the planet in the time between his ascension into heaven and his return to earth: "I will build my church, and the gates of Hades will not prevail against it." Jesus is building his church, and he does so through leaders. When he passed on the mission to his disciples, he said, "Go into all the world and preach the good news to all creation" (Mark 16:15). Matthew put it this way:

> Therefore go and make disciples of all nations, baptizing them in the name of the Father and of the Son and of the Holy Spirit, and teaching them to obey everything I have commanded you. And surely I am with you always, to the very end of the age.
>
> MATTHEW 28:19–20

The disciples immediately went to work, and the book of Acts records how they carried out their assignment. In each city, in what some call the "Pauline cycle,"[2] the apostolic teams repeated the same pattern:

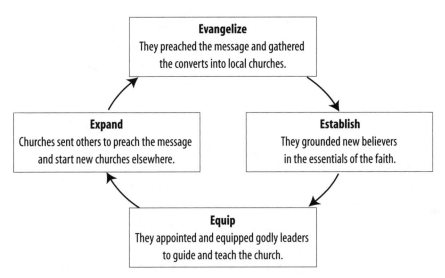

The apostolic strategy of reaching the world through multiplication was an ingenious one. It was a strategy of multiplying not just converts but local churches as well. In local churches, new believers were established in the faith and equipped to serve and lead. These churches sent out leaders to start new churches. Local churches were the leadership incubators that propelled the explosive expansion of the church from a single church in Jerusalem to thousands of churches, penetrating the known world in just a couple of hundred years.

Each generation after those earliest Christian leaders has been faced with the same challenge and opportunity. Our privilege as leaders is to reach the world through establishing healthy, vibrant churches. As we honestly assess the condition of the church in America today, most would agree that we have a lot of work to do to restore churches to their place as missional communities that effectively develop and send out leaders to multiply churches.

THE NEED

It is no secret that one of the biggest needs in the church today— all around the world—is well-equipped leadership. Just look at your own church. Would you say, "We've got all the leaders we need to accomplish all that God wants; in fact, we've got so many leaders, we've got to export the best just to make room for all the others"? We all have a strong sense that we could—and should—be doing better.

Most churches are strapped for good leadership and have no intentional strategy for developing leaders. Even many pastors feel ill-equipped, sensing that their training has not given them the competencies they need to be effective in their role.

Key lay leaders who serve on governing boards typically have little or no biblical training for their roles in the churches they are trying to lead. Youth leaders often have more training to fulfill their role than do the governing board members of the church. Yet board members are responsible for the church's overall ministry.

Some organizations that work with churches have identified tension between the senior pastor and the governing board as one of the greatest hindrances to church unity and effectiveness. Board members are typically well-meaning, but few have ever been mentored for their ministry responsibilities. Rarely has anyone intentionally focused on developing their character maturity or their theology, especially their theology of the church. Yet they are the most influential leaders in our churches. We have found that most members of governing boards would love to receive leadership training. They long to see their governing experience be more spiritual, effective, and enjoyable. Pastors would do themselves and their churches a huge favor by making leadership development a priority.

THE ANSWER HAS BEEN THERE ALL ALONG

The good news is that God is moving. Church staff members are showing an increasing awareness of the necessity of equipping leaders. They are reprioritizing their own job descriptions to ensure that leadership development is at or near the top of the list. They are seeing themselves not just as doers but as equippers. At the same time, God is raising up countless people within local churches who want to give their lives to his kingdom. God is moving in churches all around the world to equip ministers and multiply churches.

The church has a God-given capacity to engage in whole-life leadership development. It can develop godly character in its leaders, help them forge a strong theological worldview, and build strong relational and leadership skills. The local church is by design the most effective incubator of spiritual leaders on the planet.

The answer to the shortage of church leaders around the world has been there since Pentecost. The answer is this: restoring the church to the center of leadership training—which has been God's strategy all along. When the church is actively fulfilling its mission of raising up leaders for the harvest, nothing can stop it. The answer is *church-based leadership development*.

The Leadership Baton, which unpacks this answer in three parts, is written by church leaders for church leaders. It draws on insights and principles discovered by the three authors over many years of trial and error and in a variety of church settings.

In part 1 we cast a vision for church-based leadership training, highlighting the need to settle for nothing less than a leadership development culture. We show how church-based training fulfills the biblical mandate for leaders to equip their own people and builds on movements of God's Spirit in recent centuries.

Part 2 presents a whole-life approach to leadership development in your church. This learning process is *wisdom-based* ("courses"), *relationship-based* ("community"), and *personal* ("mentoring"). Its goal is to produce servant-leaders who know God ("head"), exhibit Christlike character ("heart"), and are effective in ministry and mission ("hands").

Part 3 is a series of how-to chapters that will help you apply principles of leadership development to various leader groups in your church. Chapter 7 describes a comprehensive plan for leadership development in a local church, and chapters 8 to 11 zero in on the specific training needs of governing boards, emerging leaders, pastoral staffs, and interns.

The epilogue examines such questions as,

- What is the future for churches that fully implement a church-based approach to leadership development?
- What is the future for the church-based training movement? What is God up to?
- How can churches develop creative partnerships with other churches and institutions such as Bible colleges and seminaries?
- How can churches develop a global vision as they address accreditation/recognition, technology, and partnership issues?

We pray that, as you read these pages, God's Spirit will in fresh ways open the eyes of your heart to see the power of his glorious church, and that he will inspire you to pass the baton to others who will continue the race.

To Consider and Discuss

1. How do you or your church express your mission?

2. As a church leader, how do you feel about the privilege and weight of responsibility conveyed to you with the baton of church leadership?

3. Does your church (or group of churches) experience a shortage of strong, equipped leaders? If so, what are some of the practical results of this shortage of excellent leaders?

4. In what ways is the local church strategically positioned to be an effective leadership incubator?

5. From a quick preview of the Contents page (page 9), what parts of the book are you most eager to read, and why?

Part One

VISION: THE POWER OF CHURCH-BASED TRAINING

A CULTURE
WHERE GROWING
LEADERS THRIVE

1

Jeff: Over the last decade, we've visited a lot of great churches, trying to learn everything we can from each of them. Yet one visit stands out from all the others. For one thing, this church is in Hawaii. It was tough to make the sacrifice to go to Hawaii, but I felt particularly led by God to do so. That church visit changed forever the way I will think about ministry.

New Hope Community Church in Honolulu, pastored by Wayne Cordeiro, has a strong leadership development culture. The church had only been in existence for eight years when I visited it, yet some ten thousand people worshiped at New Hope each weekend. Most of these people were not just attenders; they were engaged participants. One of the church's basic principles is *teamwork*. Every ministry is carried out in teams, and every leader works with four other people to do a ministry that each person has a responsibility to develop and encourage. They refer to these teams as "fractals." One "surf dude" guy I met on the beach went to New Hope. I asked him if he was on a ministry team. He replied, "Of course. We do ministry as team. I'm on the evangelism fractal in the surfing ministry." I was amazed that he could describe his role that clearly. He then gave more detail about his role, telling me that he was on a team with a leader who was encouraging him but that he also had a team and a few people he was encouraging. Another lady I met also went to New Hope and was on a team that made leis for newcomers.

When I got to the church, I was amazed to see thousands of people serving with great joy. One person I talked with said he was shadowing a cameraman, learning how to be a cameraman himself. He explained that every ministry leader is encouraged to have someone in his or her shadow. Nearly everyone I met knew their role in ministry and was both being developed and developing others at the same time.

I came back from Hawaii full of enthusiasm to adopt New Hope's way of doing teams and developing leaders. I announced to our staff that we were going to do "fractal teams." I painted a great vision of how this could work. Yet, the initial attempt flopped. I made the common mistake of getting excited about a particular church's way of doing things and immediately trying to introduce it into my own church culture. Here's what I discovered: If the culture isn't ready, even the best ideas and strategies are doomed to failure. Before we try to import new ideas, improved systems, and high-quality tools for doing better leadership training, we first need to prepare the soil in our church. We need to do the hard work of embedding new values deep into our church culture.

The churches doing the best job of leadership development are not necessarily those with the best systems or tools. What each has done well is embed the value of leadership development deep into their church culture. Leadership development has more to do with who they *are* as a church than with what particular things they *do*.

PREPARE THE SOIL

Last year my wife and I grew tired of our overgrown bushes and shrubs and hired some people to rip them out. Then I began to price how much new plants would cost, and I couldn't believe it!

Why would anyone pay $100 for a dinky little plant—especially when you need about twenty of them! I bit the bullet, though, and paid the bill.

I decided to save a little money by planting everything myself, but I wanted someone else to prepare the beds for planting. When we got the estimate, the figure was astronomical! They wanted hundreds of dollars just to take out the old dirt and put in new dirt. *Dirt is dirt*, I figured. Our new plants would just have to find a way to grow in the soil we already had. I wasn't going to pay for new dirt.

A year later the results are mixed. A few plants have thrived and some have died; most are somewhere in between. Maybe all dirt *isn't* the same. If I had it to do over again, I would *prepare the soil*.

What does it mean to prepare the soil in your church so that leadership development can thrive? Over the past several years, we've learned several essential principles for cultivating a culture in which growing leaders can thrive. You can try to grow leaders without these, but your results are likely to be mixed at best. For best results, it pays to prepare the soil.

SEE PEOPLE WITH FRESH EYES

As we try to help our church cultures make the transition to be more leadership development-friendly, we must first change something within ourselves. If we are going to make the transition from *acquiring* great leaders to *developing* great leaders, then we must adopt a different view of the people in our churches. Ultimately, leadership development is as simple and organic as one person believing in another and building into his or her life. To do so, one must have the heart of a developer. We have to view people much differently from the way we naturally would. We must put on the eyeglasses of *potential*.

Jeff: I got my first pair of contact lenses when I was fourteen. On the ride home from the optometrist's office. I could see everything so clearly. Clouds had shape and texture; the sky wasn't just a swirl of blue and white. Trees had individual leaves; they weren't just green blobs on brown sticks. The new lenses helped me see the world differently.

The prerequisite to becoming a developer of leaders is putting on a new set of glasses, what I call "the eyeglasses of potential." The heart of a developer sees not just who a person *is* but what this person *can become*. This painting by René Magritte, a French painter who lived in the early twentieth century, captures the heart of leadership development:[3]

The artist's subject is an egg, but this isn't what is appearing on the canvas. He sees beyond what the egg is to what the egg will become. Seeing people through eyeglasses of potential means looking beyond the actual to the potential in someone's life. At some point, someone saw you that way and gave you an opportunity to lead. That person believed in you probably more than you believed in yourself.

Jeff: When I was a young teenager, a college student named Todd took an interest in my life. You'd probably never have put us together just by looking at us. I was "preppy," and he dressed as though the hippie movement had never ended. He had wild hair, flare-bottom jeans, and a big leather strap around his wrist. Yet he was passionate about Jesus Christ and was wearing the eyeglasses of potential when he saw me. I was just a young absentminded kid, but he saw something more than that. He challenged me to do big things for God as a young student and initiated a mentoring relationship. He taught me and a few others from the Scriptures and coached us as we assumed increasingly challenging ministry responsibilities. He never let us look down on ourselves because of our youth, to paraphrase the apostle Paul's words to Timothy in 1 Timothy 4:12.

I'll never forget the night Todd took me to a nice restaurant for dinner—something he had never done before. He had with him a letter he had written me, and he handed it across the table. This is what it said:

> Jeff, when I look at you, I see a lion cub. You are young, playful, fun to be around. A lion cub. Yet when I really look at you, I see more than a lion cub. I see a lion. I see someone who has such leadership strength. I see someone whom God is using and will use to do incredible things for him. I'm just glad I get to see the lion cub becoming the lion.

What do you think he did for me as a young teenager? Todd gave me a vision for my life that was much bigger than I would have come up with by myself. Though the letter was damaged in an arsonist's attempt to burn down our church offices, twenty-five years later I still have it—and it still brings me encouragement.

Imagine what would happen in your church if leaders viewed everyone in the church through the eyeglasses of potential. When the church's core leaders make it their habit to constantly look for people's potential, this mind-set will likely spread throughout the whole church.

CAST DOWN THE IDOL OF EXCELLENCE

Jeff: To prepare the soil for effective leadership development, we need to challenge a value that has become prominent in many churches over the last decade—the value of excellence. Over the last years, many churches have greatly improved their church programming to better reach unchurched people and to honor God in worship. Megachurches especially have worked hard to implant the value of excellence into their church. I understand the lure of this value. One of our ten core values at Fellowship Bible Church North is "Excellence in Ministry." Yet, taken too far, an emphasis on excellence can cancel out the value of leadership development.

Recently Rick Warren, senior pastor of Saddleback Valley Community Church in Lake Forest, California, challenged me to think carefully about this as he facilitated a small group of pastors in a discussion about how to build an equipping church. He said that, if you want to build an equipping church, you have to tear down the idol of excellence. Why? Because most people are not excellent; most people are not extraordinary. Most people are ordinary. If you're going to do ministry through ordinary people, you have to give up the notion of excellence.

If your highest value is excellence, then you aren't going to entrust ministry to ordinary people. You are going to go out and find the very best people. You probably won't risk putting a developing person into a significant role either, because you don't want to compromise excellence. You won't give away ministry to lion cubs, and you won't work with eggs.

In *The Good Enough Church*, Steve Sjogren, pastor of Vineyard Community Church in Cincinnati, Ohio, argues that good enough is good enough. We don't have to wait until we can be excellent before we can do good stuff. Only a few—by definition—can be extraordinary. God calls us to do the best we can with what he has given us.

REWARD EQUIPPERS OVER DOERS

As you work to build a culture of leadership development, remember that you will create in a church what you model. You will also create what you reward. Many of us naturally reward doers. When faced with a problem or an opportunity, these self-starters roll up their sleeves and make things happen. In a culture that values activity, such people are the ones who get promoted and praised.

In a culture of people development, those who get rewarded are not the ones who "do things" but those who "empower other people to do things." They see it as their role to equip other people. If you want to deepen this value of leadership development in your church culture, look for ways to reward it.

Recently we initiated a new award for leaders at Fellowship Bible Church North called the "Jim Harris Servant Leader Award." The award was created to honor the late Jim Harris, a godly man who was for many years a board member and pastor at the church. When we give out these awards each year, we communicate what we value. If we only honor individuals who are out doing ministry, it's not a bad thing, but we may be missing an opportunity to further instill this core value.

Rex and Merlene were among the first to receive the Jim Harris award. This couple has done an outstanding job in building a team of people to host our newcomer events each month. They model how to encourage and equip others while doing ministry together. Honoring such people reinforces the value of leadership development.

How should we evaluate the effectiveness of our staff pastors? In Ephesians 4:11–12, Paul says that God gives us pastors whose task is to equip God's people for the work of ministry. If we evaluate pastors primarily on how well *they* are doing ministry as individuals, we are emphasizing the wrong criterion. More important are questions like these:

- How well are our pastors equipping others to do ministry?
- How many people have they empowered to do ministry?
- Are they doing ministry through a team?
- How successful are the people around them?

Give Every Leader a Baton

Jeff: A couple of times a year at Fellowship, we host a leadership orientation workshop for new and emerging leaders. During this workshop each new leader receives a baton that is inscribed with "2 Timothy 2:2." When we give it to them, we say: "We are giving you this baton, but it is not for you. The baton is for someone else. It is for you to give away. Begin praying now for the person you will develop to take your role one day. When you give it away, ask us for another baton. But remember, that baton won't be for you to keep either."

It is not uncommon for new leaders to come to leadership orientation carrying the batons their ministry leaders gave them. It has been astounding to see how powerful the affirmation of receiving a baton has been. It is a way of saying, "I believe in you. God has put something in you that is really unique, and he has done it on purpose. God is going to use you."

Recently I used the baton illustration while speaking to a group of pastors. As I packed up to leave, one of the pastors began sharing with me about some challenges he was experiencing in his church. I was about to put the baton in my briefcase, but I decided to give it to him instead. I honestly wasn't thinking much about the gift; I just thought he might be able to use it in his ministry. As I handed him the baton, I could tell he was deeply moved. His eyes began to tear up, and he said, "Really? You want me to have this?" Then I realized the opportunity God had given me to encourage him, and I said, "Yes, absolutely. God has really gifted you, and he is using you right now. Hang in there and keep serving your people. You're doing a great job."

He walked out of that room different from when he came in. I did, too. I realized once again the power of affirmation. All of us desperately need people to believe in us, to name in us what God has put into our lives to use for his glory. The more you can empower every leader in your church to be on the lookout for other leaders to whom they can pass the baton, the more people you will have stepping up to the leadership plate.

Empower every leader to be on the lookout for his or her replacement. Train your leaders to develop prospective leaders through coaching, mentoring, and encouragement. Either figuratively or literally, give every leader a baton. And when one person passes the baton to another, be sure to celebrate!

When you give every leader a baton, you will identify a wider variety of future leaders. I, for example, tend to be most excited about visionary, enthusiastic, entrepreneurial types. I can easily overlook other personality types that have an equally exciting leadership potential. But since we empower all of our leaders to be on the lookout for potential leaders, they often choose people whom I or other pastors hadn't even considered, people who then become some of the most effective leaders in our church.

GROW PEOPLE WHERE GOD HAS PLANTED THEM

Strong leadership development churches usually hire from within rather than from the outside. Often you can get up to speed more quickly by tapping the outsider. Yet it often happens that this new person doesn't fit in very well in a church with a unique and well-defined culture. More often than not, you will be miles ahead in the long run by hiring someone from within who has been exposed to and developed in your own church culture.

Churches that place a high value on developing incredible programs over developing people will tend to identify and pursue the brightest and best in the country. The advantages are real; however, so are the disadvantages. By hiring an outsider, you may well be communicating that, when you really want to do something great, you are going to go out and find the best rather than develop the best internally. There is a huge difference between leadership acquisition and leadership development.

Jeff: The Dallas Arboretum has an impressive display of flowers from all over the world. My wife loves going there from time to time just to see God's creativity and beauty. For her it's an opportunity to worship. To keep these plants healthy and growing takes an amazing number of staff people. Their job is to take plants that are not designed to grow well in North Texas and make them flourish—not an easy task, by any means

Another part of the arboretum, however—the "native North Texas" section—takes very few people to keep it looking great. All the plants there are native to North Texas, and therefore they thrive naturally and with very little help. They flourish where they were designed to be planted.

In the past, many church leaders who wanted to do ministry better hired the most extraordinary people they could find to come in and make their churches beautiful. This was an expensive and often very difficult process. Today more and more churches are looking to their native soil, where they find people who have proven in earlier ministry roles their character, their fit with the church's culture, and their faithfulness. These churches see such choices as not just the safest ones but also the best ones. Surely there are times when we need to hire from outside—times when it's the most appropriate thing to do. Yet, the more you can hire from within, the more you'll reinforce a culture that values leadership development. You will also raise up new leaders for the kingdom rather than merely transferring leaders from somewhere else.

GIVE PRIORITY TO LIFELONG LEARNING

To build a culture devoted to training others, we must be growing ourselves. We never arrive at a place where we're only developing others. If we want others to prioritize learning, then we must as well.

Jeff: As pastors and elders, we make lifelong learning a priority. One way we do this for our pastors and elders (for us in separate meetings) is to set aside two hours twice a month for ongoing development. At times we have resource people come and share. Other times we discuss a book or a particular church model. Often we'll go through courses produced by the Center for Church Based Training that are well designed for such training.

When I became pastor of leadership development at Fellowship, I was asked to lead the discussions with both groups. Gene Getz, the senior pastor at the time, wanted someone else to facilitate so that he could participate along with his fellow elders and pastors. What was interesting—and a bit unsettling—was that Gene had written many of the articles we were reading. How was he going to handle our critiques of his own articles and books? At first I was intimidated to lead with Gene Getz there as part of the group, but he made it so easy. Gene is one of the most voracious learners I've ever been around, and he jumped right into the critique of his own work. He was a learner among learners. In reality, he was the most open learner of them all, which communicated volumes to the other elders and pastors.

As senior pastor, Gene also modeled the priority of leadership development. For the first few years, we met weekly as elders and pastors for two hours each time. When you added the preparation time of two hours to the four hours he was involved in these courses (since he was the only one who attended both the elder and pastor studies), he was the most committed of anyone. In light of his own busy schedule, he took away from everyone the "I'm too busy" excuse. Ongoing development was either a priority, or it wasn't. When we asked our leaders at Fellowship to make their own development a priority, we weren't asking them to do something that Gene Getz and the other elders and pastors weren't doing themselves.

THE VISION OF CHURCH-BASED TRAINING

We aren't suggesting that churches merely add a few leadership development tools to their current church programming. What we are proposing is much more radical: that churches do the harder and more fruitful work of building the *core value* of leadership development into their church culture. Only then will such tools and concepts flourish in our churches.

The church is the vehicle God has chosen to use to raise up leaders for his work in the world. Over the past centuries, we have allowed the church to move to the sidelines, and we are now lamenting the results. Churches all over the world suffer from a serious leadership vacuum. We know, though, that local churches can and should be the most productive soil in which to grow leaders. Doing what we are describing in this book is not easy, but it is central to our mission as Christians. Participating in the process of building churches that build leaders is potentially the most fruitful and fulfilling work you will ever do.

Imagine looking back at the end of your life and seeing one or five or twenty people who are doing great things for God, and realizing that you played a part in developing and deploying them. Imagine looking back and realizing that you helped a whole church become an equipping church, where hundreds or thousands of people are fulfilling their calling in God's kingdom as a result. Imagine looking back and seeing not just one church but two or ten or a hundred churches that were birthed in large part because of a passionate effort to raise up new leaders for the mission. Imagine seeing thousands of people who came to know Jesus Christ as a result of these leaders' ministries. This is the vision of church-based training.

This vision can be realized in your church if you are willing to let the Holy Spirit plant the value of leadership development deep into your own heart and then into your church's culture, restoring the central role of the local church in the process of leadership development.

To Consider and Discuss

1. How would you assess your current church culture? Is the soil well prepared to develop and empower new leaders?

2. Why is it important to "prepare the soil" for leadership development in a church? What might it look like to prepare the soil in your church?

3. Who has viewed you with "eyeglasses of potential"? Share a story of one person who helped you see who you could become with God's help.

4. How effectively is your leadership team modeling leadership development and a commitment to lifelong learning?

5. To what extent have you seen the "idol of excellence" become a barrier to leadership development?

6. How do you respond to the concept of rewarding "equippers" more than "doers"?

7. Do you agree or disagree with the idea of hiring from within? Why?

8. Why do you think church-based leadership development is potentially so powerful?

An Emerging Movement

2

Bruce: My passion is developing leaders. In 1988, Lanier Burns, chair of the systematic theology department at Dallas Theological Seminary, asked if I would consider joining the faculty to teach theology. I was honored. In the fall of 1989 I began teaching at the age of twenty-eight. My vision was to train a generation of leaders over the next forty years as a professor of theology. It was not to be.

I love the local church. And I enjoy long-term relationships and the challenges of building a team to accomplish a great mission. At the end of each semester, I hated to say good-bye to students with whom I had only had a relationship for fifteen weeks.

During my first year at the seminary, I heard about church-based training from Jeff Reed, who was directing BILD International in Ames, Iowa. Jeff asked Gene for permission to translate material from Gene's books. Gene was interested in this vision of church-based training, and he asked me to work with Jeff and make a plan for implementing church-based training at Fellowship Bible Church North.

Church-based training brought together my passion for developing leaders with my love for the local church. By my second year on the seminary faculty, I was beginning to realize that seminary teaching was not the best use of my gifts. Yet I was reluctant to leave. *If I left, would I ever have this opportunity again?* I wondered.

As it turned out, God stepped in and moved me. Finances were low. Cuts had to be made. So I was asked to change from full-time status to an adjunct role. Although this move was painful and not one that I chose, I now see how it benefited both me and Christ's kingdom. I shifted from developing leaders in a school setting to giving myself to developing leaders in the local church.

The phrase "church-based training" and variations of it have become increasingly popular labels for reforms in leadership development. In some circles the phrase is fast becoming a buzzword, which means it may also be losing content as it gets applied to more and more diverse forms of training. In this chapter we want to bring some clarity to the concept without trying to draw exclusive boundaries.

Church-based training offers an approach as old as the Bible and as fresh as the latest training trends, so why is it emerging now? How did the church move away from the center of the leadership development mission in the first place? How does church-based training relate to other training trends? To fully understand what church-based training is all about, it helps to see it against the backdrop of history and in the context of recent movements. With broad brushstrokes, we will put church-based training on the map of history, and then place it in the context of some contemporary trends.

FIRST-CENTURY LEADERSHIP DEVELOPMENT

How did we go from the vibrant, dynamic development practices of the Lord Jesus and his passionate disciple Paul to our academic schooling model that restricts senior church leadership to degreed professionals? A fresh look at the biblical record reveals a deceptively simple and amazingly powerful approach. Both Jesus and Paul invested their lives in a few key leaders. Both drew people around them to whom they could pass the baton of leadership.

Both were effective in mentoring emerging leaders in the context of doing ministry to build competence and sound doctrine. Yet for both, *building character* came first. In Paul's advice on choosing church leaders (1 Timothy 3; Titus 1), the central issue is character. Paul's emphasis on character echoes Jesus' own focus on godliness in the Sermon on the Mount (Matthew 5–7) and Jesus' interaction with the disciples on humility and servanthood (see, for example, Mark 10:35–45; John 13:1–17).

Jesus and Paul share several refreshingly simple and remarkably profound principles for developing leaders. They both developed their leaders

- in the midst of doing ministry;
- in pursuit of an earthshaking mission;
- with a focus on godly character;
- in the context of a small team—building relationships and community, sharing "life on life";
- with time for reflection on ministry experiences;
- over a long period of time, and assuming continual learning;
- and with a greater concern for faithfulness and obedience than for knowledge and skill.

A quick review of church history shows that we have shifted from these dynamic leadership development practices of the first century. How did this happen? Why are most of our training approaches so different from that of Jesus and Paul?

A VERY BRIEF HISTORY

MONASTERIES (500–1300)

From the apprenticeship, "in-ministry" model of Jesus and Paul, monasteries arose as the Roman Empire fell. In early medieval Europe, most leadership training moved away from local churches (and their gospel mission) to monasteries, where monks carefully protected and copied ancient scrolls. In monasteries, priests developed nonprofessional future leaders in close communities where they fostered individual devotion to God, but this leadership development was largely separated from the life and ministry of the local church.

UNIVERSITIES (1300–1800)

With the birth of the Renaissance and then the invention of the printing press in the middle of the fifteenth century, monasteries gave way to universities as new centers of learning. Instead of priests helping young leaders develop their spirituality, learned professors in universities taught young men academic, dogmatic theology. Hundreds of young men memorized questions and answers from Saint Thomas Aquinas's *Summa Theologica* as they sweated in preparation for lengthy oral exams in Latin. Though universities did an admirable job transmitting the deep knowledge of that day, the emerging leaders, while very knowledgeable, were often unskilled in practical church ministry.

SEMINARIES (1800–PRESENT)

A desire to increase the skill level of ministers was one reason behind the emergence of seminaries in eighteenth-century America. The momentum away from first-century style in-ministry training continued as formal graduate schools were founded to prepare people to be professional ministers. On their campuses they assembled the new ministerial trainers, usually Ph.D. specialists in specific academic fields. For most of the twentieth century, a seminary degree functioned as the ticket for entrance into formal church leadership.

As seminaries multiplied and matured, they took on two often competing tasks: (1) to give students a classic academic grounding in theology and (2) to train students in practical ministry skills so they could function well as professional ministers. The fundamental tension between serving as a serious scholarly academy and a professional vocational institute led to many internal struggles in seminaries between the "academic" and "practical" departments.

	Monasteries	Universities	Seminaries
Keepers of Knowledge	guard scrolls, copy manuscripts	library of all existing books, protect ancient documents	specialized library of books, journals, and other media
Trainers of Church Leaders	priests, monks	learned professors, generalists	Ph.D. specialists in specific fields
Strength	community, spirituality	knowledge of all fields	expert knowledge and professional skills

WHERE WE'VE LANDED TODAY

The full professionalizing of Christian ministry that began in the European universities was completed in American graduate-level seminaries. Many people now believe that a paid church leader must have a seminary degree. At the same time, they assume that church board members don't need any serious training.

Most seminaries today are aware of their limitations and are trying to do something about it. Limitations in character formation are being addressed through various small groups, faculty mentors, and courses on spiritual formation. Limitations in providing ministry experience are typically tackled with field education and internships. Limitations in developing relational skills are handled by personal counseling sessions and by encouraging ministry involvement outside the school. Limitations in audience are being addressed through degree programs that appeal to a broad spectrum of people. However, systemic problems inherent in the nature of schools as they now exist make dealing with these serious issues challenging.

Retired theology professor Edward Farley asks pointedly, "How [did] something born in the migrations of an ancient, nomadic, and tribal people, and at the bloody scene of a crucified Jew and the fiery tongues of Pentecost, [end] up with classrooms, degrees, libraries, universities, Sunday schools, and teaching elders?"[4] Indeed, how have we moved to such a radically different way of training leaders, so different from biblical patterns?

We believe that separating the preparation of church leaders from local church ministry and mission, combined with the pressures of academic respectability and professionalism, has damaged Christ's church. Local churches have both neglected the training of leaders within the congregation and largely abdicated to professional schools the responsibility for training pastoral leaders—and this has had profound consequences for the church:

- Insufficient numbers of competent, godly leaders are being developed for local churches.
- Local churches are often pragmatically driven without deep theological underpinnings.
- Many governing board members are unequipped to shepherd the church.
- The mission of Jesus Christ is compromised.

These realities must be faced head-on by courageous leaders. For the sake of Jesus Christ, we can no longer look only to the current system of ministerial preparation to provide leaders for our churches.

Local churches need spiritually mature leaders who are called by God and who are experienced in real day-to-day church life. Our local churches need devoted men and women who can apply practical biblical wisdom to crucial issues and who can seize kingdom opportunities with faith and love.

CURRENT TRAINING TRENDS AND MOVEMENTS

Certainly we are not the first to identify these concerns. Many concerned leaders have written critiques of current approaches to theological education and ministerial preparation. Some leaders have noted the massive changes in our culture and in our churches that drastically alter the landscape for training new church leaders. The following selected training trends arise from these shifts and contribute to them. Together these training trends invite us to reconsider first-century style leadership development—training that takes place in the midst of ministry, training that is concerned with character, and training that is compelled by Christ's mission. We need an approach rooted in vital community (sharing life-on-life) as we pass on quality biblical learning. These trends are calling us back to the centrality of the local church in the leadership training process.

SMALL GROUP MOVEMENT

Starting in the 1970s, churches began forming small groups to meet the needs of pastoral care, adult education, and community. The breakup of families and our mobility as a society have contributed to an epidemic of isolation that has created a deep hunger for relationships. For many people, small groups are a support structure that substitutes for their extended family, from which they are separated by distance or divorce. Yet many church small groups remain largely social gatherings characterized by loose fellowship without focused discipleship.

The small group movement has generated a huge market for small group Bible study materials. It has ignited an explosion of six inch by nine inch stapled booklets on almost every imaginable topic—all with slick covers and creative interior designs. These materials have also been used in adult Sunday school classes. Each small group needs a leader, so churches have developed many innovative training programs, workshops, and seminars to equip the leaders (pastors) of their small groups. In some ways, small groups function like little churches in which the leaders serve as pastors. These leaders need ongoing training in order to fulfill their roles well.

DISCIPLESHIP MOVEMENT

Before the small group movement began, the discipleship movement was already underway. Seeing the lack of discipleship in churches, visionary leaders founded many parachurch ministries to address the need. Campus Crusade for Christ, The Navigators, and InterVarsity Christian Fellowship were among the most influential organizations shaping this movement. While they were most effective on college campuses and military bases, many of these ministries moved into discipling adults in conjunction with local churches. Trainers in this movement focused on emerging leaders' need for accountability, character development, and practical action for Christ's kingdom. In its early days, the movement, with its overly individualistic focus, largely ignored local churches. As the discipleship movement has matured, it has more actively collaborated with local congregations.

CONFERENCE AND SEMINAR MOVEMENT

Most pastors feel the need for ongoing training for themselves and their staff members. To meet this need, a new expert has arisen—the reflective practitioner. Church leaders are flocking to quality seminars, conferences, and forums offered all over the country, mostly by local churches who model "best practices." The growing recognition of the centrality of the local church is directly affecting the training of church leaders. Churches are now eagerly getting involved in developing their own leaders. The seminar movement shows the credibility of the new experts—experienced, reflective practitioners who can say, "Here's how I did it."

EXTENSION EDUCATION MOVEMENT

Theological Education Extension (TEE) took one of the first steps toward distance learning for church leaders. The genius of

TEE is in bringing quality learning to the trainee, yet the center of the enterprise remains the institution. *Extension* is the key word; the institution is extended to individuals, yet the training is not done in the context of the life and ministry of the Church. TEE represents a rethinking of the leadership training enterprise in response to the need to train those who don't have easy access to quality learning.

TECHNOLOGY

In addition to these movements, technological advances over the last few decades make specialized knowledge accessible to people on an unprecedented scale. Universities and seminaries arose and have endured largely in response to two needs—the need for a centralized library and for a centralized faculty. With the rise of the Internet, CDs, and DVDs, as well as cable and satellite technology, people today have access almost instantaneously to more information than exists in many of the large libraries. The need to actually go to a school to hear an expert give a lecture is gone. Not only are lectures available online, but students can interact with teachers by phone connection, videoconferencing, and email. Technological advances are decreasing our reliance on centralized formal schools and opening up new decentralized options for providing quality training for church leaders.

CHURCH-BASED TRAINING

This issue of leadership development may not be quite as simple as going back to the way leaders were trained in the first century. We would never endorse an anachronistic, simplistic turning of the clock back to Paul's day, nor would we ignore the value that schools and parachurch groups offer. But could it be that we've overlooked some simple but profound principles inherent in the training approaches of Jesus and Paul? Why not train leaders *in the midst of ministry* as we pursue *fulfilling the great mission* given to us by the Son of God? Why not develop church leaders with a focus on *godly character* in the context of *community* as we build close relationships with each other? Why not reflect with emerging leaders on their *ministry experiences* as we develop them over a long time, being concerned with *faithfulness and obedience* while developing *biblical knowledge and ministry skills?*

A movement among churches, parachurch organizations, and even seminaries is emerging to say, "Yes, we can!" Some have labeled this movement "church-based training." Church-based training returns to biblical patterns for leadership development while building on the strengths of the major historical models and the recent training trends.

	Monastery	University	Seminary	Emerging
Keepers of Knowledge	guard scrolls, copy manuscripts	library of all existing books, protect ancient documents	specialized library of books, journals, and other media	public domain, Internet, interlibrary loan
Trainers of Church Leaders	priests, monks	learned professors, generalists	Ph.D. specialists in specific fields	reflective practitioners
Strength	community, spirituality	knowledge of all fields	expert knowledge and professional skills	community, mission, character, skill, in-ministry model

Like the monastic model, the church-based training movement seeks to develop community and spirituality, and a spiritual adviser (pastor) is significantly involved in the process. Along with universities, church-based training sees knowledge as vital to leadership development. In accord with seminaries, church-based training focuses on developing professional skill and specialized knowledge for ministry-specific responsibilities.

Movement	From ➜	To	Core Value	Church-Based Training
small groups, care-based	loose fellowship	ordered development	vital relationships	
discipleship, campus-based	individuals	communal	personal mentoring	
conferences, event-based	event out there	process right here	ministry experience	
extension, school-based	formal, at a distance	nonformal, up close	quality learning	

Church-based training stands on the shoulders of the most recent training trends. Along with the small group movement, church-based training shares the value of community, a commitment to train lay leaders, an in-ministry development process, and a priority on building close relationships. It shares with the discipleship movement a mentoring process, a focus on character growth, a passion for evangelism, and a vision to disciple the nations. It shares with the seminar/conference movement the value of ministry experience carried by reflective practitioners as the new experts in developing church leaders, and with the extension education movement church-based training shares a desire to bring quality education to learners where they are and with their time preferences.

Not long ago leadership training was moving farther away from an in-ministry approach and farther away from the local church. Thankfully, a shift is beginning to take place. The movement today is bringing us back to a more first-century style leadership development process, retooled for the twenty-first century. The local church is reemerging at the center of the leadership training enterprise. God seems to be catalyzing a movement that returns leadership training to an in-ministry, apprenticeship, church-based model. We believe church-based training will strengthen Christ's church because it is based on biblical principles, builds on historical developments, addresses complexities of the twenty-first century, and meets the needs of today's local churches.

THE POWER OF CHURCH-BASED LEADERSHIP DEVELOPMENT

Here's how we define church-based training:

> Developing all believers to maturity and many to leadership in the local church, under the authority of local church leadership, with other churches, through an apprenticeship, on-the-job approach, for Christ's mission of multiplying churches worldwide to God's glory.

We need to seek to bring all to maturity, and then from these maturing people we need to develop many for leadership. Let's unpack the above definition.

"IN THE CHURCH": THE POWER OF CONTEXT

The training takes place in the life and ministry of the local church, which is the visible expression of the body of Christ (Acts 13:1; Ephesians 1:22–23). The church is the body of Christ, the family of God, the temple of the Spirit. The church is the hope of the world. God is at work today in a direct way through local churches.

"UNDER THE CHURCH": THE POWER OF RESPONSIBILITY

The training takes place under the authority of the leaders of the local church (Acts 20:25–31; Hebrews 13:17), who must give account to God for the training of godly leaders and for the maturity of the church's members. In developing leaders in a local church, we are working with people who have God-given responsibility for that church or for a specific ministry in that church. In Acts 20:28 Paul told the elders of the church in Ephesus that they were responsible for the flock over which the Holy Spirit had made them overseers, responsible for the local church that Jesus Christ purchased with his own blood.

In the churches we serve, our leaders realize that God holds all of us responsible for how we use what we're learning to improve our church's ministry. This direct accountability to God gives church-based leadership development an energy missing from most classrooms.

"WITH OTHER CHURCHES": THE POWER OF PARTNERSHIP

Churches need both autonomy and interdependence, as in the first century (Acts 11:22–24). Rarely does one church by itself have all the necessary resources for developing leaders, but we can and should work together locally and globally to develop leaders.

"THROUGH THE CHURCH": THE POWER OF COMMUNITY

The training takes place through an informal, in-ministry approach to maturity and leadership development (Acts 11:25–26; 2 Timothy 2:2). This kind of leadership development involves much more than just offering courses. It is a *process* built into the very fabric of a local church's life and ministry. This is not a little Bible institute that operates alongside the church and meets in a Sunday school classroom. Church-based people development occurs in and through the real-life, ongoing ministry activities of a local church. It includes life-on-life mentoring in the context of real community.

"FOR THE CHURCH": THE POWER OF MISSION

The training takes place for the sake of the lost and for the multiplication of the local church worldwide (Acts 13:1–5; 14:21–28). We are not just learning for the sake of learning—which only leads to pride and sterility. We are developing leaders for the sake of reaching people for Jesus Christ in our community and for the sake of multiplying churches around the world!

"TO GOD'S GLORY": THE POWER OF WORSHIP

Ultimately our goal is to develop people for the purpose of bringing glory to God the Father, Son, and Holy Spirit (Romans 15:5–6; 2 Thessalonians 1:11–12). When you are serving Almighty God, it changes your perspective. We should develop leaders, not just because it's an effective way to run our ministries, or even because it's the right thing to do, but because we want to bring honor and glory to our God.

NOTHING CAN STOP THIS!

Jeff: Shortly after the fall of Communism in the Soviet Union, I was discussing church-based training with a man affectionately known as "the Duke," who was at that time the leader of the Baptist Union in the Ukraine. He was quite a leader, having endured incredible persecution and imprisonment in the Communist era. By then, his diabetes and other ailments from his time spent in work camps had made him physically very weak, but he radiated a spiritual dynamism and vitality. After listening to me for a while, he suddenly became highly animated when he realized that I wasn't talking about missionaries coming to teach in the churches but about handing the process of leadership development over to the churches themselves. I was suggesting that the church itself become the soil in which leaders are intentionally and yet naturally grown. He leaned over his desk and exclaimed, "Nothing can stop this. If you really hand [leadership development] over to the churches, then nothing can stop this. We could train all the leaders in the Ukraine. What could possibly keep us from doing so?"

The Duke was right. The answer to the leadership vacuum we see around the world is to restore the church to the center of leadership training. This has been God's strategy all along. When the church is fulfilling its mission of raising up leaders for the harvest, nothing can stop this!

To Consider and Discuss

1. What characterized leadership development in the New Testament?

2. What lessons can you draw from this chapter's brief look at the history of church leadership development?

3. How have you personally been involved in some of the current training trends and movements? What strengths and weaknesses do you see in them?

4. How does church-based leadership development build on these trends?

5. How would you define church-based training? Interact with the definition provided in this chapter. What is clear about it to you? What is unclear?

6. What are some ways in which church-based training can benefit your church?

Part Two

PROCESS: A WHOLE-LIFE APPROACH

Designing
a Leadership
Development
Strategy

3

Rowland: In *The Seven Habits of Highly Effective People,* Stephen Covey asks you to imagine being at your own funeral. Four speakers are scheduled to say something about you. "What would you like each of these speakers to say about you and your life?" asks Covey.[5] Rather a morbid thought, but it got my attention. I realized that I wouldn't care much whether people talked about my achievements. What really mattered was that my wife, family, and close friends in my church community would remember me as a mentor who loved Christ passionately and loved them unconditionally. That insight helped me to think strategically about my mission in life.

Have you ever stopped to think *strategically* about developing leaders in your church? The word *strategy* is made up of two old Greek words—*stratos,* which refers to an army or large group of people, and *egy,* which comes from the verb "to lead." Around 500 BC a senior commander in the Athenian army was called a *strategos,* and the whole army was led by ten *strategosi,* who were elected by their fellow citizens.[6] They were chosen for their ability to think well. Strategic thinkers determine the most important long-term goals, then develop plans to reach the goals.

STRATEGIC GOALS:
START WITH THE FINISH LINE IN MIND

Are you intrigued by the possibility of your church cultivating a leadership development culture (chapter 1)? Are you convinced that the local church must be central in developing your leaders (chapter 2)? Then you may be tempted to reach for an off-the-shelf leadership development program for your church. Before you do so, ask: "What kind of leader do we want to produce?" A reflex reply could be "A Christlike servant-leader." A more comprehensive answer might be "A Christlike leader whose 'head' [a wise leader], 'heart' [a Spirit-led leader of sterling character], and 'hands' [a skillful servant-leader] are functioning in harmony.

It might pay to consider the kind of leader we *don't* want to produce. Imagine a body with an inordinately big head. Some church leaders are like this. They know so much. They use their biblical knowledge like a club to pummel followers into submission. In Paul's words to the members of the Corinthian church, they become "puffed up" with pride in their superior knowledge (1 Corinthians 8:1).

A body with a massive heart, skinny limbs, and a pea-sized head would look equally absurd. Church leaders with overly enlarged hearts typically exude compassion and emotion but care little about doctrine. When there is some difficult task to be done in the church, they duck for cover. Yet, a torso with massive legs and arms, a pea-sized head, and a faltering heart is just as defective. Some church leaders serve themselves into the ground while neglecting sound doctrine and spiritual formation.

In designing your model for leadership development in your church, keep this goal in mind: By God's grace, we want to produce wise leaders who are sound in their knowledge of God's Word and his world, strong in character and compassion, and skillful in ministry and mission.

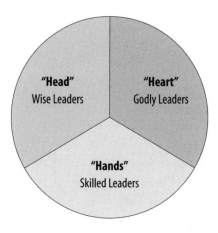

HEAD: LEADERS WITH GODLY WISDOM

Paul told Titus that church leaders had to hold firmly to the message so they could encourage others by sound doctrine and refute those who oppose it (Titus 1:9). Our leadership development strategy must include opportunities for existing and aspiring leaders to grow in their knowledge of God and of the Bible. This knowledge needs to go beyond mere mastery of facts to cultivation of biblical wisdom.

HEART: LEADERS WITH GODLY CHARACTER

At its core, leadership is influence. Godly influence doesn't arise from titles; it flows from an intimate knowledge of God. Christlike leaders are in touch with the Spirit of God and steeped in the Word of God. Paul put it this way to a leader-in-process: "Train yourself to be godly. For physical training is of some value, but godliness has value for all things, holding promise for both the present life and the life to come" (1 Timothy 4:7–8).

Your church may have busy leaders, powerful leaders, authoritative leaders, even successful leaders, but if you don't have leaders with godly character you are in big trouble. Settle for nothing less than leaders who have Christlike character and compassion.

The decisions of Captain Edward J. Smith on the fateful night when the "unsinkable" *Titanic* went down revealed deeper character flaws.[7] Less than one year earlier, Smith had been in an embarrassing collision with the *HMS Hawke*. Soon after that he damaged his ship by sailing it over a submerged wreck. With his new ship, *Titanic*, he wanted to patch up his flagging reputation. He set a crazy speed for the ship. Policy required him to have "moderate speed and maximum comfort," but he wanted to prove a point and treated the *Titanic* like a sports car. His overconfident attitude became apparent when he boasted to his dinner guests that the ship could be cut into three segments and each would float.

Captain Smith was a leader, but he was a leader with a flawed character. In our churches, we need to be developing leaders with godly character. They may never come face-to-face with an iceberg, but they will face crises that will reveal their character strengths and weaknesses.

HANDS: SERVANT-LEADERS WHO EQUIP OTHERS

When James and John asked for the top spots in his kingdom, Jesus countered, "You know that those who are regarded as rulers of the Gentiles lord it over them, and their high officials exercise authority over them. Not so with you. Instead, whoever wants to become great among you must be your servant, and whoever wants to be first must be slave of all" (Mark 10:42–44). Christlike leaders are primarily servants. The world system is into domination and power plays. The citizens of this new community, the church, influence others by sacrificially serving them.

In *Servant Leadership*, Robert Greenleaf shares that the inspiration for his book came from *Journey to the East*, a book written by Hermann Hesse that tells the story of a group of men on a journey.[8] Leo goes along as the servant who does the menial chores, but who also encourages the group with his spirit and song. He is a person of incredible presence. Everything goes well until Leo disappears. Then the group disintegrates and the journey is abandoned. They found they couldn't make it without the servant Leo. Years later, one of the party came across Leo, who turned out to be the head of the group that organized the journey in the first place.

Leo illustrates one facet of biblical servant leadership—the willingness to take the lowest place. Ephesians 4:11–12 identifies another: Church leaders don't settle for merely doing the ministry (without paying attention to threats to the mission of the group); they *equip* others to serve God well. When they leave the group, it functions effectively because people have been prepared for service.

STRATEGIC COMPONENTS: EQUIP IN A WHOLE-LIFE CONTEXT

The second strategic question church-based developers of leaders must address is this: "How can we provide a rich context where whole-life development can take place?" In one sense, *we* don't develop leaders; God does. By his Holy Spirit, he trains and shapes and molds his leaders. But we can provide an interlocking framework (rather than a formula) to optimize the development of the leaders in whose lives God is working.

A whole-life approach to growing leaders will benefit from three integrated strategic components: courses, community, and mentoring.

COURSES: CULTIVATE BIBLICAL WISDOM

It's easy to roll out a one-liner like, "Courses don't train leaders, people do." It's easy because it sounds so right—right, that is, until your strategy includes the cultivation of biblical wisdom as a vital goal for your leaders. If your aim is to produce Christian leaders who think wisely and well, then courses that encourage theological reflection are an essential component in leadership development.

The overall goal of producing wise, godly, and skilled leaders should drive the choice of course material. Consider this checklist as you choose leadership development courses for your church:

- Do these courses encourage whole-life development?
- Do these materials allow the participants to formulate their own biblical convictions?
- Do these courses facilitate the development of a learning community?
- Does this curriculum provide an ordered pathway for leadership development in our church?
- Does the design of these courses incorporate effective methods of adult learning?

Rowland: Jenny and her husband, Ben, were small group leaders in our church who faced a series of serious family crises in a short space of time. They were enthusiastic members of a theology course I was leading called "Discovering Intimacy with God." Soon after one of their kids had run away from home, Jenny said to me one night, "Rowland, I'm so thankful we studied the lesson 'Our God Is Sovereign.' That truth was like an anchor when our family was drifting onto the rocks." Courses that encourage theological reflection and bring about life-change provide stability for existing and emerging church leaders.

Community: Facilitate Relational Learning

Learning takes place best in community. Jesus modeled this as he trained the Twelve. He spent time with individuals, giving extra attention to Peter, James, and John, yet he taught his twelve disciples mostly as a group. When he needed to speak unvarnished truth to them, he did so in front of the others. For example, when an argument broke out among the twelve disciples about who was the greatest, Jesus sat them all down—even though James and John's mother had tried to promote her boys—and said, "If anyone wants to be first, he must be the very last, and the servant of all" (Mark 9:35). Then he sat a little child on his knee and taught all of them more about humility in the kingdom of God.

If it's true that learning is optimized in community, then we should view any regular meeting of a ministry team, leadership group, or study group as an opportunity for the "one anothers" of Scripture to take place. Rather than viewing these occasions as meetings for only decision making or study, we should elevate them to become communities of love where we can build each other up and communities of truth where we can be honest and open with each other.

A community approach to leadership development in the local church implies that we are choosing to love. We are committed to each other. We are family. And it is an organic process.

MENTORING: ENCOURAGE SPIRITUAL FRIENDSHIPS

Christian mentoring is a purposeful spiritual friendship to encourage growth in both the mentor and the protégé. Essentially it is a friendship between two or more people who respect each other. Mentoring is *spiritual* in the sense that it needs to be orchestrated by the Holy Spirit and result in spiritual transformation. Mentoring is also *purposeful*. Going to lunch with somebody is not in and of itself leadership development. But enjoying lunch together can provide the occasion for intentionally asking developmental questions about the knowledge base, character, and ministry skills of your protégé.

Because mentoring is at its essence a friendship, forcing people into mentoring partnerships seldom works. Rather, we need to hold high the value of intentional spiritual friendships, model what it means to be a spiritual father or mother, and provide opportunities for God-directed mentor links to take place.

Courses, community, and mentoring may sound like a leadership development formula, as though you can develop godly leaders by enrolling them in well-designed courses ("head"), then encouraging body life ("heart"), and finally tacking on some mentoring relationships ("hands"). In reality, all three of these strategic components should occur simultaneously.

Courses provide opportunities for authentic community and meaningful mentoring to take place. When genuine community occurs among leaders, mentor links will occur naturally. And when intentional spiritual friendships are formed, gaps in the leader's knowledge, character, and ministry skills will be identified and filled. Most important, courses, community, and mentoring provide a rich and varied context in which whole-life development can occur.

STRATEGIC PEOPLE: IDENTIFY KEY GROUPS TO BE TRAINED

The third strategic question church-based equippers need to ask is this: "Who are the most committed leaders in our church, and how will we develop them?" It is strategic because many churches take their leaders for granted and easily adopt a haphazard approach to leadership development.

Who are these highly committed leaders? They include the following:

YOUR GOVERNING BOARD

What are you doing to develop the "head," "heart," and "hands" of these highly committed people? Are you offering them stimulating courses and regular experiences of authentic community? Are peer-mentoring relationships developing among them? Leadership development needs to begin with your leadership core.

YOUR STAFF

What are your plans to enhance the development of your staff members? A strategic plan (involving courses, community, and mentoring) should be in place for your paid as well as your unpaid leaders. How are you helping them grow as leaders? If you have interns, are you merely "using" them, or are you developing their gifts and passion for ministry?

YOUR EMERGING LEADERS

What about the many leaders immersed in such ministries as leading small groups, working with children and teens, or leading other ministry teams? Have you formulated plans for the whole-life development of this highly committed group? Have you assessed their individual developmental needs and then customized a program for each of them?

Stephen Covey's question about what we'd like people to say at our funeral helps us think strategically about our lives. What would you like Jesus to say about your God-assigned task of equipping leaders when you stand before him on his Day of Review (see Hebrews 13:17)? Consider your leadership development strategy. If you start with the finish line in mind, equip others in a whole-life context (expanded on in the next three chapters), and identify key groups to be trained, it may be your joy to hear, "Well done, good and faithful equipper!"

Think through three strategic goals—

STRATEGIC GOALS	"HEAD"	"HEART"	"HANDS"

using three strategic components to achieve the goals—

STRATEGIC COMPONENTS	COURSES	COMMUNITY	MENTORING

with all three groups of strategic people.

STRATEGIC PEOPLE	GOVERNING BOARD	STAFF	EMERGING LEADERS

To Consider and Discuss

1. Why is strategy important?

2. As you start with the finish line in mind, what kind of leaders do you want to develop at your church?

3. In your church, do you focus more on "head," "heart," or "hands"?

4. Why is context important for developing leaders?

5. How do courses, community, and mentoring all play a role in building a rich, whole-life context?

6. Which leader groups in your church would be most strategic in terms of focusing your leadership development efforts?

7. Where do you think your church needs to invest the greatest effort in designing an overall approach to developing leaders—defining strategic goals, developing strategic components, or identifying strategic people?

Courses: 4
A Wisdom-Based
Learning Process

COURSES COMMUNITY MENTORING

Bruce: It was my first day as the new college pastor. I saw Mike and Jimmie in the back of the room with Mickey Mouse hats on, daring people to say something. Yet, at a deeper level I saw "potential leaders" written all over their faces. A few months later I met their friend Vinny, a muscular man with long, wild hair and a giant chip on his shoulder. He scared me. Vinny came to faith in Christ on a college retreat and underwent a radical transformation.

I didn't know what to do with these three modern-day disciples. I didn't have a road map showing me how to develop leaders, nor had I ever heard of church-based training, but I knew I had to do something.

My wife and I often invited Jimmie, Mike, and Vinny into our home. I involved them in serving and later in leading the college ministry. We tried "spiritual boot camps"—short periods in which we enforced strict spiritual disciplines, including various kinds of fasts. We tried working through discipleship material inside fat notebooks titled "Equipping the Saints."

Although it didn't happen right away, in time all three became hungry to serve Christ through full-time professional ministry. I realized that, while they needed knowledge, they also needed character formation and ministry skill. They needed to know how to learn for a lifetime.

Through BILD International, I discovered church-based training resources for potential leaders that emphasized wisdom over knowledge and character over facts. These resources went beyond asking learners merely to fill in the blanks to teaching them to think. I began creating materials to help Jimmie, Mike, and Vinny learn to think and study for themselves. We grew deep bonds of friendship as we shared life together, whether through playing chess, handling a crisis in the group, or planning our next outreach event. Mike, Jimmie, and Vinny were there for the births of three of my children. They watched us up close and personal. We learned and grew together.

As they grew as leaders, they joined the Fellowship internship program—which I personally had gone through and was directing at the time. As these men worked with other pastors in various ministries beyond the college group, we continued to work our way through church-based training courses. The day they came before the elder board for ordination was a special day. Having completed their course work, performed significant ministry, and given evidence of godly character, we ordained them for ministry (without seminary degrees!).

Although we didn't realize it at the time, as I worked with Mike and Jimmie and Vinny, through trial and error the Lord led us into a healthy, exciting leadership development process that would have potential far beyond the training of these three men.

OUTCOME DRIVES DESIGN

When I began looking for training resources for these three men, I knew it wasn't enough to find materials I could trust doctrinally. I knew Mike and Jimmie and Vinny needed to become wise leaders who could think well biblically about the crucial issues of this day. I got that much right. But it didn't occur to me to consider the educational design of the resources.

Over the years I've learned that, because the method typically determines the outcome, educational design matters tremendously. What kind of leaders do we want to develop? Smart leaders? Skillful leaders? Wise leaders? Your outcome—the kind of leaders you want to develop—should determine the educational design of your training resources.

We need to cultivate practical biblical wisdom in our future leaders. Sadly, cultural trends are dumbing down our society. Image is replacing substance; sound bites are crowding out editorials. We are content with superficiality. In the church world, many, if not most, seminars and conferences focus on what works—giving participants the skills and know-how to create efficient systems for youth work, small groups, and church plants. Functional skills for measurable results this year are the demand of the day, but could it be that we are shortsighted? While skills are important, if we don't cultivate higher-level thinking and mature wisdom, what will happen to our churches over time? Without theological depth, our numerical "success" may be short-lived. Practical skills, no matter how finely tuned, do not fully equip leaders for the complex and subtle challenges that local churches have faced since Pentecost.

If better skills are not enough, perhaps more knowledge would help—and it might—but the crying need in our day is not for more information. We are drowning in information, overwhelmed with more data than we can possibly digest. Future leaders must develop more than a vast store of knowledge. To guide our churches well in the twenty-first century will require leaders who can exercise practical biblical wisdom. We're not talking about the rare sages or seminal thinkers, although we need them, but about the ordinary local church leaders who serve God in week-to-week ministry.

A LEADERSHIP DREAM

Our dream is to see churches raise up thousands of wise leaders— men and women who can think well about the multifaceted issues that confront us. Imagine local churches led by teams of people who can bring theological depth to practical problems, who can see into knotty issues and resolve complex crises. If we want this outcome—wise leaders who can think biblically—then we must be intentional about the educational design of our training materials.

Can a particular course or curriculum guarantee that it will produce leaders who exercise practical biblical wisdom? Certainly not. However, we'd be foolish to suppose that our educational approach does not have an impact on the kind of leaders we develop. A wisdom-based approach is much more likely to generate deep, thinking leaders than a fill-in-the-blank, "fill your heads with facts" approach.

A WISDOM-BASED PROCESS

As adults most of our thinking consists of problem solving. Few of us have the time or inclination to be philosophers wracking our brains over ancient philosophical puzzles and conundrums. On the other hand, we all wrestle with practical decisions every day. Some of these decisions involve important theological issues. For instance, a wife asks if she must obey her husband when he tells her not to take the kids to the doctor because there's no money to pay for it. Her dilemma raises theological questions about submission and the nature of marriage. It raises questions about a mother's responsibility to her children. It forces her to compare the value of physical health to the importance of obeying her husband and the desirability of avoiding debt.

None of these issues are located in the philosophical classroom. They are the nitty-gritty concerns of a real woman with real children who may need to see a doctor. Life has a way of forcing us to address tough questions. How do we answer the compelling questions life places before us? We need to learn how to think biblically. Leaders in Christ's church must develop practical godly wisdom, not only for their own sakes, but also for the sakes of their people who bring challenging situations to them, and so they can wisely navigate the many churchwide issues every local church faces.

Whether the issue is a marriage conflict or a debate about church government, a personal ethical choice or a theological position, good thinking involves a similar process.

A WISDOM-BASED DEVELOPMENT DESIGN

While we certainly don't claim to have found *the* method that works best for all people at all times, we are delighted with the way the "Six-Step Wisdom Process" has changed lives in our churches and many other churches around the world. This six-step approach to learning draws on insights from Scripture, classical tradition, scientific research, and contemporary culture. (For a fuller account of influences that contributed to formulating this wisdom process, see appendix 1.)

This six-step framework provides the educational design for most of the courses written by the Center for Church Based Training.[9] It doesn't work with every subject. For instance, learning Greek requires memorizing and quizzing; learning to preach requires supervised practical application (practicum) with evaluations. In most subject areas, however, we've seen great results from using this approach. People in our churches are not just learning content or gaining skills; they are learning how to think biblically. They are becoming wise.

This six-step process does not and cannot stand alone. A comprehensive approach to training leaders must also include such elements as mentoring, reflective experience, and community. We learn best when we learn in a variety of ways—from listening to lectures to learning by modeling. Plus, optimum learning strategies vary with a person's age, learning style, and the subject matter.

Recognizing these limitations, let's go on to identify the six-step process:

1. *Grasp the issue.* Come to understand the problem.
2. *Study the Scriptures.* Look to the Bible as your authority
3. *Consult other sources.* Seek counsel from wise people.
4. *Form a response.* Formulate your point of view.
5. *Discuss the issue.* Test your view with others.
6. *Take steps to obey.* Act to address the issue.

1. Grasp the Issue

To think wisely, we must first grasp the issue. While this seems self-evident, it is less than simple. Grasping the issue involves *exploring* the problem. Is the surface disturbance the real issue, or are deeper forces at work? Whether in a counseling situation or a philosophical debate, we must develop good skills at observation and discernment. We must first realize that a problem exists before we can make a conscious effort to solve it. Sometimes we're not even aware there is an issue until an explosion rocks our world. Since adults learn best when they are addressing an issue or solving a problem, if we are serious about creating a context for learning, it's helpful at first to uncover a problem or issue.

From the very beginning of the process, every step must be bathed in prayer. As Christians, the Holy Spirit—the Spirit of truth, the Spirit of wisdom—lives in us. When we face difficult situations, our first response should be to get on our knees, and then we need to stay in touch with God throughout the process.

Exploration leads to *expression*. The multiple dimensions of most real-life issues can lead to confusion and frustration. Psychological, doctrinal, relational, and financial concerns, all intertwined, create an emotionally charged atmosphere in which it can be difficult to think skillfully. At this stage we must try to state the essence of the controversy. As the twentieth-century economist/journalist Henry Hazlitt insightfully observes, "A problem properly stated is partly solved."[10]

In expressing an issue we work to dispel vagueness and avoid confusion. We try to determine the essential elements of the dispute or issue and then articulate the precise problem.

Example

Let's say we decide to study the issue of parenting. Using our wisdom-based approach, we'd begin not with a presentation summarizing the topic but by seeking to grasp the issue. What key questions need to be explored in order to develop a biblical understanding of parenting? Some possibilities include the following:

- What does a godly parent look like?
- Should we all be parents?
- What are the duties of a parent? When do these duties end? How do they change over time as your children grow older?
- Do fathers and mothers have the same, or different, roles in parenting?
- What aspects of parenting cross all cultures, and what aspects should be shaped more by the specific culture?
- What difference does it make if you are a good parent or not?

Many contemporary Christian authors teach that your family should take priority over your ministry; in contrast, authors in previous centuries emphasized the need to sacrifice for the sake of Jesus Christ—including sacrificing your family. Who is right? What is the right balance?

Mini Case Study

Bob and Alice serve as missionaries in a developing country. Their young daughter, Mary, suffers from chronic health problems. The level of available health care for Mary's condition is primitive in the country where they minister. If they were to return home to their sending country, Mary would receive much better care, but they are having an effective ministry and feel called to be with this people group. What should the family do?

Sound Bites

- "As parents your children are your highest priority. Everything must come second to them and to their needs."
- "Parents should not let their children be the center of the family, controlling its priorities and affairs."

State the Issue

In one sentence express the issue we are addressing.

_____

_____

2. Study the Scriptures

Having grasped the issue, where do we go to find answers? To the Bible. God has not left us without truth but has graciously revealed to us his own thoughts. We want to train people to go to the Bible with every issue in their personal lives and church ministries. We have seen men and women who, after working through these steps a number of times, encounter problems and immediately ask, "What does God's Word say about it?"

Frequently an issue will require a study of several passages and multiple principles.

Example

Study the following passages and list enduring biblical principles for parenting:

Deuteronomy 6:1–9 _____

Psalm 127 _____

Ephesians 6:1–3 _____

What can we learn from the negative example of parenting in
Eli's life (1 Samuel 2:12–36; 3:11–14)?_____

3. Consult Other Sources

There are a number of proverbs in the Bible that point to the
wisdom of consulting advisers (11:14; 15:22; 20:18; 24:6). Advisers can take many forms. We may read commentators on key passages that are relevant to the issue at hand. We may seek the advice
of older godly people who have experience with this specific type
of situation. We may read books and articles on the issue or listen
to cassette tapes, watch DVDs, and search electronic databases or
utilize online services. Sometimes historical studies will be helpful, as we draw on the wisdom of the ages from other godly leaders who have faced similar problems in previous centuries.
Sometimes non-Christian scholars will be helpful because we seek
information from other disciplines to help us grow in wisdom. For
instance, a controversy may involve legal dimensions and thus
require advice regarding current case law.

Example

Read a chapter on parenting written by Kent and Barbara
Hughes.[11] Evaluate what you read according to the teaching of
Scripture. What do you agree with? What do you disagree with?
Why? (In our typical CCBT courses we provide outstanding
excerpts from the best authors on each topic.) Of course, other
advisers do not have authority equal to Scripture. We do not agree
with every line of every reading we supply in our CCBT courses.
We want to train church leaders to think biblically, to evaluate all
other input against the Word of God. In this case, we want to learn
from the Hugheses, but we also should be critically evaluating their
point of view biblically.

4. Form a Response

After grasping the issue, studying the Scriptures, and consulting multiple advisers, we go on to formulate a possible response. Life often forces us to make decisions within time frames outside our control. As responsible shepherds, Christian leaders are frequently called on to share their wisdom, and they seldom have the luxury of asking for six months to study the issue.

At this point in the process, we want to form a tentative response, not a final, refined, carefully worded conclusion. This is the time for creativity. We should produce many ideas, deferring our critical judgment for a while. Look at the issue or problem from as many angles as possible. Challenge the obvious.

A response can take many forms. One possible response is simply to pray. We may write out a position on the issue. We may form action plans to change things in our own lives, families, or churches. Any response will involve making decisions and choices regarding the matter before us.

Example
- Write out a list or description of biblical parenting principles, limiting yourself to those that are cross-cultural. Try not to let your own cultural perspectives color too heavily your reading of Scripture.
- Evaluate your own parenting (or preparation for future parenting) against the biblical principles. If married, discuss your evaluation with your spouse. Pick one area to work on for improvement.

5. Discuss the Issue

Our wisdom is often greatly enhanced when we test our initial responses in the community of faith. Share your response with other godly leaders who are wrestling with the same issue. Together sharpen each other. If you can work on an issue as an elder team or a special task force, you will gain greater wisdom than if you tackle the issue on your own.

A focused discussion of an issue by a group of leaders who have all been working on the issue ahead of time can be an exciting occasion. Together, prepared leaders indwelt by the Spirit of truth will generate a synergism in which ideas and wisdom will be produced far beyond what any one person could create alone. Together, guided by the Spirit, we can see a wider, more expansive horizon. We sharpen, challenge, and confirm one another.

Example

Have a leader facilitate a discussion on the issue of parenting. If you are leading the group with this six-step approach, you have many tools to draw on to foster a great discussion. You could use the opening questions under "Grasp the Issue," or you could ask the group to address the case study or respond to the sound bites. Open the Scriptures and ask the learners to compare their lists of biblical principles. You could pursue the implications of one particular Bible passage. In addition, you can turn to the Hugheses' article and guide an interaction with their thoughts. In a typical CCBT course we'll provide you with a list of discussion questions that tie the learning elements together. As a group the point is to gain deeper wisdom on parenting together than you would grasp by yourself. Your initial conclusions in "Form a Response" will be confirmed, challenged, and sharpened by the group.

6. Take Steps to Obey

Having tested your initial response in discussion with other wise, prepared leaders, you then can go back and refine your response. Sometimes you'll end up fine-tuning what you thought was a wise approach. Other times you may scrap your first response and start fresh. In any case you will have gained greater wisdom and confidence from testing your response in a community of leaders. Adjust your first response in light of the wisdom gained from the group.

Knowledge should never stop in our heads but should move us to action. Jesus called us to teach people to obey everything he commanded (Matthew 28:20). If we are hearers only and not doers, we deceive ourselves (James 1:22). Truth and wisdom only come to fruition in obedience.

Example

Refine your list of biblical principles based on the discussion. Then, by yourself or in conversation with your spouse, take one action this week that will make you a better parent by applying (at least) one of the biblical principles with your children.

THE FRUIT OF THE PROCESS

Bruce: Where are Mike, Jimmie, and Vinny now? Mike has helped develop a junior high ministry at another church, served on a city council, and been involved in a church-planting ministry. Because of his training through many church-based courses (without formal training in a Bible college or seminary), Jimmie can think theologically and practically about complex ministry issues. He now serves with me as one of the pastors at McKinney Fellowship Bible Church. Vinny served as a pastor with Fellowship Bible Church North and on the staff of the Center for Church Based Training. Today he works as a consultant for churches and businesses, helping people develop leaders according to their style of influence.

While at Fellowship, I once had the opportunity to simultaneously teach both graduate courses at Dallas Theological Seminary and church-based training courses at the church. While students in the school were motivated, their immediate goal was a good grade. In contrast, leaders in our church were vitally engaged because the future of our church was at stake. They knew they were responsible for the direction of the church and for her mission.

About two years into our church plant, I led a group at McKinney Fellowship Bible Church through a course on missions. While we had set aside 10 percent of all general fund giving for missions and had generously supported various missionaries and groups, we had no clearly defined criteria for evaluating the requests we received for support. People were asking us what we were going to do and not do, and why. I invited our elders and other church members who were excited about missions—potential leaders of a future global ministries team—to participate in a course in the spring. The goal of the course was to shape a long-term direction for missions at our church.

Meeting around a conference table in an elder's title company office, we engaged in hours of lively discussion as we tried to figure out God's direction for global missions at our church. Sometimes our discussion became animated as we wrestled with what activities constituted mission. Do hospitals qualify? Do our activities in our own city qualify? What about working with local people who speak another language? These were just some of the questions we labored over. We always left as friends, but we often went home with unresolved questions to be picked up the following week.

Group members wrote brief papers outlining their views as to how we should approach such matters as integrating evangelism and social concerns. People photocopied articles they wanted the rest of us to read. By the end of the course, we had drafted a direction paper that laid the foundations of our McKinney Fellowship Bible Church Global Ministry. This foundational work led to creating a global ministry team made up largely of people who had gone through this course together.

Why was this such a powerful process? Many reasons, but this was a key: Each person felt personally accountable to God for the direction and health of the church. As we opened the Scriptures, the issues were far from dry and academic. At each point we asked each other how we were doing personally in our obedience and how our church was measuring up, based on what we were seeing in God's Word. Then we faced the questions of what changes we needed to make in our lives and in our church in order to be honoring to God. Fresh convictions were formed. Real change took place. Two years later, our church has a thriving global ministry, involving many new leaders, that has grown directly out of this study.

The educational design of your materials makes a great difference in the kind of leaders you produce. What should you look for in your training materials? We suggest you look for resources that

- go beyond teaching knowledge to cultivating wisdom, character, and ministry skills;
- reflect a high view of the authority of Scripture;
- are designed for use in a community setting rather than in a classroom lecture setting or in an independent study format; and
- encourage lifelong learning in the context of community.

We need more than skilled leaders, more than knowledgeable leaders. We need wise, godly, competent leaders who possess the judgment skills to be able to distinguish the best from the better and the permanent from the fleeting. The challenges facing the twenty-first-century church require thousands of wise leaders who can do practical theology in real life.

To Consider and Discuss

1. How do desired outcomes influence educational design?

2. What kind of outcome do you want in the leaders you are developing?

3. In what ways have you seen life require wisdom more than knowledge or formulas?

4. What are some ways that beginning with "grasping the issue" can improve the learning process?

5. Why is it important to study the Scriptures first when you confront an issue?

6. Why not just stop with the Bible? What is the value of consulting other sources?

7. What value does group discussion add to the process above and beyond what could come from working through a course alone?

8. Why is it significant for the learning process to result in obedience?

9. How would you evaluate this six-step wisdom process? How could it be helpful for the leaders you are developing?

COMMUNITY: 5
A RELATIONAL
LEARNING PROCESS

Wayne Cordeiro, pastor of New Hope Community Church in Honolulu, Hawaii, makes this compelling observation about community:

> Community happens when there's a sense of relationship, regardless of the activity. It happens when each gathering takes on the atmosphere of a family reunion, where hugs are abundant and bursts of laughter come easily. It happens when people enjoy just being with one another and where the atmosphere is more than just friendly.[12]

Is this how you would describe the relationships in your leadership team? Do your elder meetings have the flavor of a family reunion? Are your ministry team meetings focused more on the tasks at hand or on relationships among members?

Rowland: One time as an elder I was assigned the task of redesigning our church's small group ministry to encourage a deeper level of genuine *fellowship* (the word we used in those days). In an elders' meeting I suggested that we elders needed to look at the level of fellowship among ourselves before we tried to raise the relational temperature in the church as a whole. I'll never forget the looks on the faces when one elder blurted out, "I agree. We're friendly, but we're not friends!" Some looked shocked, but most of us were relieved that someone had finally said what we were feeling.

GOD PRIZES COMMUNITY

Community, in the sense of intimate fellowship and close companionship, has been eternally true of the Triune God—Father, Son, and Holy Spirit. Theologian Stanley Grenz puts it this way:

> As the doctrine of the Trinity indicates, the one God is the social Trinity, the community or fellowship of the Father, Son and Spirit. Because God is a plurality-in-unity, the ideal for humankind does not focus on solitary persons, but on persons-in-community. God intends that we reflect the divine nature in our lives. This is only possible as we move out of isolation and into godly relationships with others. Consequently, true Christian living is life-in-relationship or life-in-community.[13]

God's commitment to life-in-community is captured in Psalm 133:

> How good and pleasant it is
>   when brothers live together in unity!
> It is like precious oil poured on the head,
>   running down on the beard,
> running down on Aaron's beard,
>   down upon the collar of his robes.
> It is as if the dew of Hermon
>   were falling on Mount Zion.
> For there the LORD bestows his blessing,
>   even life forevermore.

This psalm was written by one of the Bible's greatest leaders, King David. Maybe he was reflecting on the joy of unity in Israel after all the years of being hounded by King Saul (2 Samuel 5:1–10). Maybe Psalm 133 is a tragic commentary on the opposite in his life—those times when he experienced disaster, distance, and disunity in his family (2 Samuel 12–24). Whatever the occasion, the psalm celebrates the joys of close community.

Authentic community is "living together in unity." It is like a family in harmony. And it is "good and pleasant." Church leaders must settle for nothing less than genuine community. When church leaders emphasize the priority of community and consistently model it, their example will shape leaders-in-training and the whole congregation. The level of community in any group will reflect the level of community modeled by the group's core leaders. It was true in King David's day, and it is true in ours as well.

Psalm 133 concludes: "For there the LORD bestows his blessing, even life forevermore." Where genuine community exists, God is pleased to pour out his blessings. The accent here is on God's initiative—*"the LORD commanded the blessing"* (NASB, emphasis added).

If you want God to breathe life into your leadership development, start where God starts and love what God loves—authentic, loving community among the leaders—then watch it flow to other leaders and to the entire church body.

THE CHURCH IS A COMMUNITY

For all the talk about the church as the people of God, our language betrays us. We talk about the number of churches in our district—and invariably refer to the buildings. We talk about "going to church" as though church were a place or an event.

Biblically, the church is God's called-out people-in-community. It is God's new community, where dividing walls such as race and status have been demolished (Ephesians 2:11–22). Stanley Grenz writes, "The community of love which the church is called to be is no ordinary reality. . . . Our fellowship is nothing less than our common participation in the divine communion between the Father and the Son, mediated by the Holy Spirit."[14]

As a fellowshipping people, these truths shape our life together:

- Barriers that once existed between Jew and Gentile, rich and poor, slave and free, have been abolished by Christ's work on the cross (Galatians 3:28; Ephesians 2:14–16).
- Reconciliation has been extended through Jesus Christ being made sin for us on the cross (2 Corinthians 5:21).
- We still experience conflict with each other, but on the basis of the walls crumbling and reconciliation being extended, we gladly forgive fellow sinners. As Matthew 18:21–35 teaches, greatly forgiven sinners forgive greatly.

If the church is at its core a closely knit community of love, a less-than-perfect community of forgiven sinners, what does this mean for leadership development? We need leaders who embody what the church is. We need leaders who are passionate about modeling community and who are committed to developing other leaders in the context of community.

JESUS TRAINED THE TWELVE IN COMMUNITY

Mark 3:14 captures Jesus' training method: "He appointed twelve . . . that they might be with him and that he might send them out to preach." Note the words "with him." Evangelism professor Robert E. Coleman summarizes Jesus' training methodology in these words:

> For the better part of three years, Jesus stayed with his pupils. They walked the highways and streets together; they sailed on the lake together; they visited friends together; they went to the synagogue and temple together; they worked together. Have you noticed that Jesus sel-

dom did anything alone? Imagine! He came to save the nations—and, finally, he dies on the cross for all mankind; yet while here he spends more time with a handful of disciples than everybody else in the world."[15]

To me this sounds a lot like learning in community!

So close were the Twelve to Jesus that while the word *disciple* is found in the gospels around 225 times in relationship to his followers, he applies this term to the Twelve on only two occasions (John 13:35; 15:8). He favored expressions for the Twelve that indicate heart-bonding: "my brothers" (Matthew 12:49; 28:10; John 20:17), "children" (Mark 10:24), "friends" (John 15:15; 21:5) and "my friends" (Luke 12:4). Jesus didn't form a school; he majored on developing close relationships with the Twelve and then sending them out to serve.[16]

Jesus trained his disciples through the experience of a loving community, but he also developed them by immersing them in the wider community. His was no cozy leadership development club; it was a community that existed for the lost, lowest, and least.

Evaluate your present leadership development strategy in light of Jesus' approach to training the Twelve in community:

- Do you select leadership trainees after extended times of prayer?
- Do you train leaders in small groups?
- Have you built close friendships with your leaders-in-training?
- Do you take leaders-in-development with you wherever you go?
- Do you send out your trainees to do ministry as a key aspect of their training?
- Do you involve your trainees in ministry among the lost, lowest, and least?
- Do you ask questions more often than give answers?
- Do you regularly debrief trainees so that they learn from their successes and failures?

GROWING LEADERS
BY CREATING EXEMPLARY COMMUNITIES

As Psalm 133 hints, community must be lived out before it is lectured on. Budding leaders need to observe seasoned leaders enjoying community together. They need to see the "one anothers" of Scripture lived out on a daily basis. Do these "one another" commands describe your leadership team?

- *Be members of one another (Romans 12:4–5; Ephesians 4:25).* Does each person feel like part of the team? Do you affirm that you need each member?
- *Be devoted to one another (Romans 12:10).* Have you expressed a covenantlike commitment to each other?
- *Accept one another (Romans 15:7).* Do you accept other team members for who they are, not for what you would like them to be?
- *Instruct one another (Romans 15:14).* Do you gently, yet firmly, teach and warn fellow leaders who are going off course?
- *Greet one another (Romans 16:16).* Do you notice each other and find appropriate ways to express intimacy?
- *Carry one another's burdens (Galatians 6:2).* Do you know each other well enough to share burdens?
- *Encourage one another (1 Thessalonians 5:11).* Do you regularly speak words that put wind into the sails of team members?

What are some practical ways you can nurture such relationships within your leadership and ministry teams?

INVEST TIME TOGETHER

Rowland: We need to plan activities that are designed to build community. Once our elders' group got over the shock of acknowledging that, in reality, we were not friends, we scheduled a luncheon one Sunday a month. For six months we gathered in the spacious home of one of the most hospitable elder couples I've ever met. Sometimes it was "couples only"; other times we brought our children. Our elders' team was transformed from a cold, businesslike group into a family—and it all started with something as simple as eating together regularly.

Wayne Cordeiro calls community the gel that fuses hearts together. He tells the following story:

> Some years ago in Hilo when we were in the middle of our building program, we purchased a 20-acre lot; and after a few years, we raised enough money to begin building. I recall the day we poured the cement for our fellowship hall. It was an area larger than that of a high school gymnasium, so this was no small task!
>
> Fifty men gathered at early dawn on a Saturday. We each wore a pair of rubber boots and the oldest, most disposable clothes we could find. The trucks began arriving at 7:00 a.m. The sun rose like a golden disk, watery at first, but then it began burning our skin as the morning wore on. Beads of sweat rolled off our foreheads, only to be mixed into the concrete. . . . After completing the project, we kicked off our boots and sat in huddles, summarizing the events of the day. We laughed, chided each other, and relived every minute of the pour, over and over and over again. By the time we had washed our trowels and headed home, it was dark.
>
> Looking back on that day, the most endearing memories I have are not of the pour itself but, rather, what happened between our hearts during the pour. We arrived as brothers in Christ, and by the end of the day, we left not only as brothers but also as friends. The pour was not an end in itself but a means of something more eternal.[17]

ATTEND TO THE SPIRITUAL

If our leadership teams are to become healthy communities, we also need to be intentional about the shape and tone of our meetings. In his book *Transforming Church Boards into Communities of Spiritual Leaders*, Charles Olsen highlights the importance of including worship in our leadership meetings.[18] This simple addition can transform a sterile meeting into a spiritual oasis.

Rowland: One of my favorite memories is my time of service on a board that loved to sing. (It helped that we could create five-part harmony!) We would pray, sing, attend to an item on the agenda, thank God for his wisdom, sing again, laugh about some trivial matter, attend to more business, and so on. In the process we would accomplish more in one meeting than in the multitude of more "serious" meetings I've attended. We were like a band of happy siblings. More important, we were functioning like spiritual leaders. Rather than the sense of dread I sometimes experience when my calendar tells me an elders' meeting is coming up, I couldn't wait to attend those gatherings.

Allow No Clouds

Leadership teams must keep short accounts with each other. God commands all believers to accept (Romans 15:7), instruct (Romans 15:14), and forgive (Ephesians 4:32) each other. In nurturing such grace-filled relationships, leaders are to lead first by example. As less-than-perfect individuals, church leaders will sometimes sin against each other. The temptation is to allow small sins to fester in the hope that grievances will resolve themselves over time. A better way is to address the hurts promptly and honestly—to apologize when wrong and, when wronged, to extend forgiveness in light of God's amazing forgiveness.

Rowland: One time a friend knocked on my front door and said that one of my elders was spreading a rumor that I had treated my next-door neighbor badly; he said it was damaging my reputation as a pastor. The issue was whether I had paid my share of the cost of a fence between our properties. I went to my neighbor and to the builder to find out if they were upset with me. To my relief I found they were more than satisfied with the amount I had paid. My next call was to the elder who had started the rumor ball rolling. He was embarrassed and admitted that he'd gotten his facts wrong. We reconciled, hugged, and prayed. To this day, this elder is one of my dearest friends.

What effect would it have on your leader-trainees if they saw your leadership team as an "allow no clouds" fellowship of greatly forgiven sinners?

GROWING LEADERS BY CREATING LEARNING COMMUNITIES

We must root our leadership development efforts in the concept of learning in community. The Six-Step Wisdom Process (outlined in chapter 4 and further explained in appendix 1) allows for disruptive community to take place—in the sense of an environment where ideas can be challenged honestly and graciously. All church leaders face issues that have no easy answers. Step 1 *(Grasp the Issue)*, through the use of sound bites and case studies, allows for dissonance to be introduced to the issue at hand. Steps 2 and 3 *(Study the Scriptures* and *Consult Other Sources)* restore equilibrium to the learning process. Step 4 *(Form a Response)* encourages leaders to formulate their own initial conclusions. Step 5 *(Discuss the Issue)* creates opportunities for dissonance (where different views are shared frankly) and closure (where participants formulate a group response to the issue). Step 6 *(Take Action to Obey)* allows individuals and the group to revisit their conclusions and take steps to obey God's truth.

One of the great advantages of this six-step method is that it takes place in a small group rather than in a lecture or classroom setting. For years, the Fellowship elders' team and their wives (including Gene and his wife, Elaine) have met regularly, separate from their business meetings, to study together by using this Six-Step Wisdom Process. Earl Lindgren, a longtime Fellowship elder says, "When I think about the meetings we held in an elder's home, with food on the table, a coffee cup in the hand, and dynamic discussions using the six-step process, I realize that learning-in-community took place. I would describe it as something supernatural, as though the Holy Spirit delighted to be present when, as church leaders, we met in unity to learn and grow together." His words remind me of Psalm 133:3: "For there the LORD bestows his blessing, even life forevermore."

Church leadership developer Reggie McNeal says, "The leader prepared for the challenge of the new century will be a learner. However, this learning will develop differently than in traditional methods that are linear, didactic, privatized, and parochial. Learning in community is non-linear, layered, and experiential. It is also just in time."[19] McNeal draws a distinction between learning clusters—groups of leaders who get together to think out loud, hammer out approaches to ministry, and run ideas by each other—and intentional learning communities. He maintains that learning clusters become communities when a personal dimension develops among group members.

This development of relationships can be encouraged by the use of written materials that are designed to deepen community. For example, one of the lessons in the *Life Development Planner*[20] asks participants to read an excerpt from Robert Clinton's book *The Making of a Leader*[21] and then construct timelines that show how God has shaped them through various chapters of their lives. When the group meets, each leader presents his or her timeline. These presentations are invariably charged with emotion, as leaders describe the peaks and valleys God has brought them through. Almost without fail, leadership groups that complete the *Life Development Planner* bond together.

Courses without community can produce leaders who are knowledgeable but not relational. Community without courses can produce leaders who are relational but not wise. Courses with community can produce church leaders who possess both wisdom and warmth.

To Consider and Discuss

1. How is life-in-community fundamental to our created identity?

2. What kinds of problems emerge in the church when vibrant community is missing?

3. How do you evaluate the level of community among your leaders?

4. How does Paul describe the kind of community that should characterize local churches? What might it look like to practice the "one anothers" in our leadership groups?

5. How would you describe the interrelationships between the church family and our individual families (single, married, and married with children)?

6. Evaluate your own relational health. How do you feel about your friendships?

7. Think about your church. What would it look like to develop leaders in the context of biblical community?

MENTORING: A PERSONAL LEARNING PROCESS

6

A chapter on church-based mentoring wouldn't have been necessary a hundred years ago. People in that era wouldn't have called it mentoring. They would have talked about an *apprentice* who learned alongside a craftsman—a mode of training that would have been so commonplace as to hardly be worth mentioning. Long before degrees and diplomas, carpenters, surgeons, and sailors employed mentoring techniques to train their successors. A tradesman-apprentice commonly spent up to five years learning not only the skills of the trade but the way of life that went with it. In eighteenth-century New England, Christian leaders such as Jonathan and Sarah Edwards regularly had one or two pastor-trainees living in their home, where the budding ministers had opportunity to observe the quality of their marriage, the reality of their spiritual life, and the demands of pastoral duties.[22]

In our day, mentoring—of the life-on-life, apprenticeship-training variety—has made a comeback in circles as diverse as business, aviation, and education. It may sound like one of those faddish words until you realize that it's really an update of one of the most time-honored and effective methods of learning.

There is something about church life that makes it easy to attend to urgent matters like planning next Sunday's worship time but never get around to matters—mentoring leaders, for example—that are critical to the church's long-term health and effectiveness. Mentoring present and future church leaders is essential, not optional. It's essential for biblical reasons. According to Ephesians 4:11–12, church leaders are to be equippers, not just practitioners. And it's essential for practical reasons. We are not going to be here forever. We must train our replacements.

Mentoring involves bringing all people to maturity in Jesus Christ (Ephesians 4:13). In this chapter, however, we are focusing on a particular aspect of mentoring in the local church, namely, the training of potential, emerging, and existing leaders.

How, then, can church leaders go about equipping present leaders and preparing the next generation of leaders? What kind of relationship between mentors and protégés will bring about the greatest growth of church leaders?

Rowland: When our son Mark was seventeen years old, my wife, Elaine, and I had the opportunity to take an extended sabbatical at Dallas Theological Seminary. The day we left Mark and our daughter, Rochelle, behind in Christchurch, New Zealand, I gave him a farewell letter. He had one ready for me as well. His letter read as follows:

> *I know this isn't much, but I just had to tell you how much I will miss you over the next year and a bit. It is probably because over the last couple of years especially, I have come to count you as more of a friend than a father.*
>
> *I'll miss not being able to talk to you about my performance after each soccer or cricket game. I'll miss not seeing you faithfully supporting*

whatever team I'm playing for each Saturday. I'll miss not having those talks about sport, or some issue from the Bible, or just any little thing.

Anyway, I know your input into my life isn't over, but thanks for all that you've been to me up to now. Thanks for encouraging me in my walk with the Lord, but more importantly, thanks for giving me lots of practical examples of a person who loves the God he serves.

My relationship with Mark has been more like a Deuteronomy 6:4–8 relationship (talking about God and his Word naturally in a variety of settings) than a formal leadership training program. There have been times of formal learning, like the time Mark was preparing for a sermon and we worked our way through Haddon Robinson's *Biblical Preaching*. For the most part, though, it has felt more like the sharing of a life than the completion of a program.

From this experience with my older son, I learned that mentoring the next group of leaders in our local churches has to be both intentional and flexible. Although I've never spelled out that I'm "mentoring" Mark, I saw leadership potential in him and have intentionally encouraged his development in this informal way.

Mentoring is an *intentional spiritual friendship*—"intentional" because it thrives on mutually agreed-on goals, "spiritual" because it has its highest achievement when we acknowledge daily our dependence on the Holy Spirit, and a "friendship" because it works best when a warm relationship is nurtured.

PRODUCING CHAMPIONS

One way of describing the mentor's role is to say that the mentor is in the business of producing champions.

In the 1992 Summer Olympic Games in Barcelona, Derek Redmond lined up with seven others in the 400-meter final. He was favored to win a medal—with a good chance for the gold. Jim, Derek's dad and number one fan, was in the stands that day. The starter fired his gun, and Derek took off in one of the best starts of his career. Nearing the halfway mark, he heard a pop. As he crashed to the track with a torn hamstring, the other runners flew past him. Within a few seconds the race was over. The cheering stopped, and all eyes turned to Redmond. He pulled himself up from the track and started staggering toward the finish line.

Suddenly a man broke past the security guards and leaped onto the track. Jim approached Derek and had a brief conversation that went like this: "Look, son, you don't have to do this."

Despite the pain, Derek responded, "Yes, I do."

Jim responded, "Well, if you're going to finish the race, we'll finish it together." They linked arms and crossed the line together to a standing ovation from a hundred thousand fans.

The process of mentoring champions consists of five phases: identification, imitation, instruction, involvement, and release.

1. Identification: A Mentor as Talent Scout

IDENTIFICATION
Talent Scout

Local church mentors must be spotters of potential. Identifying future leaders can be a deliberate process involving an extended period of prayer, as when Jesus chose his twelve disciples (Luke 6:12), or it may be a more spontaneous insight, as when Barnabas spoke up for the newly converted ex-murderer Saul. The once proud Pharisee, Saul of Tarsus, was humbled when he became a Christ-follower. He endured the embarrassment of stumbling around blind, being met by Ananias, and then receiving his sight and being baptized. Imagine Saul's feelings when he came to join the disciples in Jerusalem and sensed their reluctance to have anything to do with him. When your world has caved in, to have someone like Barnabas speak up for you makes all the difference. Luke writes, "But Barnabas took him and brought him to the apostles. He told them how Saul on his journey had seen the Lord and that the Lord had spoken to him, and how in Damascus he had preached fearlessly in the name of Jesus" (Acts 9:27).

Notice the words of healing and affirmation:

- He has seen the Lord.
- He has heard the Lord.
- He has preached fearlessly in the name of the Lord.

Barnabas was saying, "I believe in him. I will stand by him." It's easy to believe in someone when she is popular or to cheer for an athlete who has just won a trophy. It's much harder to stand up for someone when the tide has turned against him. If you seek out people when they are crushed and whisper, " I believe in you," this reveals the heart of a Barnabas. When I was a shy teenager sitting in a corner at a birthday party, a man I regarded highly came to me and told me that I had a great future in God's service. His words still motivate me today.

Every leader of a home group and every elder in your church must always be on the lookout for people who have the head, heart, and hands of a servant-leader. More important, every leadership team in your church has to come up with a list of leaders and potential leaders who are candidates for training. I find it helpful to list three groups:

- potential leaders—children, young people, or new believers who exhibit leadership traits;
- emerging leaders—people who have characteristics of a leader but who need further development; and
- existing leaders—people already functioning as leaders in some aspect of church life.

The identification phase of mentoring tomorrow's leaders deals largely with the first two groups. It is a matter of having the eyes that see a potential leader when others may not. When you are scouting out prospective leaders, Fred Smith's checklist of what to look for ("10 Signs of Potential") is worth pinning on your notice board.

1. Leadership in the past. (They have demonstrated leadership in some other sphere.)

2. The capacity to create or catch vision. (Their eyes light up when you discuss the future.)
3. A constructive spirit of discontent. (They can think of constructive ways of doing things better.)
4. Practical ideas. (They can spot things that will work.)
5. A willingness to take responsibility. (They step forward when opportunities are presented.)
6. A completion factor. (When the work comes in, it's complete.)
7. Mental toughness. (No one can lead without being criticized.)
8. Peer respect. (This doesn't reveal ability, but it can show character.)
9. Family respect. (Does the family respect him or her?)
10. A quality that makes people listen to them. (When they speak, people listen.)[23]

Have you spotted someone in your church who has the potential to make a difference in Christ's kingdom? Have you noticed someone who has that "something extra" no one else has seen? Spend extended time in prayer about this person. Then act. Write the person a note, or meet with him or her over breakfast and declare such life-giving words as, "God is going to do great things through you."

A mentor as talent scout says, "I see potential in you. I believe in you."

2. IMITATION: A MENTOR AS EXAMPLE

IDENTIFICATION	IMITATION
Talent Scout	Example

Leadership development specialists Paul Stanley and Robert Clinton identify three key elements in the mentoring relationship: *attraction* (the protégé is drawn to the mentor), *responsiveness* (there is a readiness to learn from the mentor), and *accountability* (a mutual responsibility exists between the two people).[24] These three elements add up to *respect*. An encouraging comment from someone you respect can motivate you for months.

The apostle Paul used the words *imitate* and *example* to describe the dynamics of the mentoring process:

> Even though you have ten thousand guardians in Christ, you do not have many fathers, for in Christ Jesus I became your father through the gospel. Therefore I urge you to imitate me.
>
> 1 CORINTHIANS 4:15–16

> Follow my example, as I follow the example of Christ.
>
> 1 CORINTHIANS 11:1

> Join with others in following my example, brothers, and take note of those who live according to the pattern we gave you.
>
> PHILIPPIANS 3:17

> Don't let anyone look down on you because you are young, but set an example for the believers in speech, in life, in love, in faith and in purity.   1 TIMOTHY 4:12

> You, however, know all about my teaching, my way of life, my purpose, faith, patience, love, endurance, persecutions, sufferings . . .
>
> 2 TIMOTHY 3:10–11

Imitative living was the centerpiece of Paul's training method. Author and speaker Ruth Barton observes that "Paul's leadership training program wasn't a program at all; it was a relationship in which he opened his life to those he was helping."[25] There is something freeing about this concept. Programs don't train leaders; people do. But there is also something very demanding about serving as an example for others to follow.

Many of us find it appealing, even flattering, to think that someone might be imitating us. We hit the ground with a thud, though, when we read Paul's words, "Follow my example, as I follow the example of Christ" (1 Corinthians 11:1). We have to be following Christ closely if our mentoring relationships are going to positively shape the next generation of church leaders.

Rowland: Prior to my sabbatical at Dallas Seminary, I wasn't able to be open and vulnerable with anyone other than my wife. Soon after I arrived at seminary, a fellow student named Rick asked if I'd be interested in meeting weekly for prayer and encouragement. We did so, and God graced me with the most open and healing relationship I had ever experienced. Rick was ten years my junior, but somehow it never mattered. What mattered was that we learned from each other.

My peer-mentoring relationship with Rick whetted my appetite for a similar experience when I returned home. Since that time, God has given me several peer-mentors. Currently my mentor-buddy is Steve. For years, he and I were senior pastors of similar churches. We each drove forty-five minutes to meet monthly. Usually one of us needed support, and the other gave it. I always came away hugely refreshed. I am immensely blessed that God has given me a counselor-confidant-mentor who is following Christ closely. We have a great respect for each other, and on this basis we learn from, laugh with, and encourage each other.

Living as an example for a fellow leader to follow means that we have to learn to be vulnerable, just as Paul was when he said to Timothy, "You, however, know all about my teaching, my way of life, my purpose, faith, patience, love, endurance, persecutions, sufferings" (2 Timothy 3:10–11).

I have vivid memories of the first (and last!) half marathon I ran in. I prepared for the race for over a year. I practiced by participating in several ten-kilometer events. And I had a mentor. Jim was the president of the marathon club in our town. I admired him immensely, and we were building a good friendship. Jim knew how much the half marathon meant to me, so he said, "I'd like to run with you. It would be good preparation for my next marathon." Now I knew I wasn't in the same class as Jim, but I was glad to accept his offer. It was an out-and-back course—we ran along a flat road for a few miles and then climbed a series of hills, turned around, and ran downhill. When we got to the bottom of the hill, Jim said, "You're doing great, but you probably feel like giving in." He had hit the bull's-eye. He continued, "The reason is that it's harder on your quads to run downhill. Just be patient and you'll come out all right." We ran on together, and Jim and I crossed the finish line together.

As you mentor aspiring leaders in your church, provide a model, befriend the leader-in-training, come alongside at strategic moments, dispense wisdom, affirm, and then celebrate the new leader's success. A mentor as example communicates, "I'm an open book. Come learn from me."

3. INSTRUCTION: A MENTOR AS TEACHER

IDENTIFICATION	IMITATION	INSTRUCTION
Talent Scout	Example	Teacher

Mentoring is a relational process—intensive, occasional, or life-long—involving a respected mentor and a protégé. It includes the passing on of wisdom, instruction, skills, or a preferred lifestyle for the purpose of the protégé's growth or transformation.

As a talent spotter, you should look for people who are eager to learn. As an example, you should demonstrate a hunger to acquire more knowledge. As an instructor, you have many opportunities to teach your protégé and instill a love for lifelong learning.

In-depth Study Courses

Rowland: I once led a group of ten people through a twelve-week CCBT course called "Church Leadership." Two of them showed special interest in the topic. They were like Peter, James, and John in Jesus' band of disciples—people who were putting up their hands for greater attention. The course became a springboard for more personalized learning opportunities.

I met with Harry to talk further about the unit on "The Character of a Leader." We discussed his family situation as it related to his qualifications to serve as an overseer in the church. Alan wanted to develop his skills as an elder, so we invested additional personal time on the units titled "Shepherding: Caring for the Flock" and "Shepherding: Protecting the Flock."

Ministry Tasks

When I was a schoolteacher, I balked at the job of teaching children to swim. Someone coaxed me into the task by saying, "You don't have to be a great swimmer to produce champion swimmers." I was skeptical but decided to do my best. To my surprise, I produced a couple of school champions!

As a pastor I had the privilege of coaching several preachers. My routine is simple. We work our way through a book on preaching while they are preparing a sermon. It has been exciting to see some of these preachers become better at preaching than I will ever be.

Life Experiences

If your approach to mentoring leaders in the church is more like building a relationship than checking leadership development off your to-do list, if it is more like a spiritual friendship than a spiritual contract, then teachable moments will often arise as you talk and play and work. A mentor as teacher communicates, "A love of lifelong learning is a legacy I'd like to leave you. Let's learn together."

4. Involvement: A Mentor as Coach

IDENTIFICATION	IMITATION	INSTRUCTION	INVOLVEMENT
Talent Scout	Example	Teacher	Coach

One of my professors told me that if someone were to give him a clean slate and ask him to train cutting-edge leaders for the next generation, the process would look like the training of a Boeing 747 pilot: There are times of intensive learning from books, followed by learning in a flight simulator. Most important of all, there are thousands of hours of flying. It's tempting to think we've trained future church leaders if we merely expose them to seminars on leadership. Yet we must remember that leaders learn to lead primarily by leading.

Barnabas not only spotted leadership potential in Saul, he also involved him in mission and ministry. Luke records the enviable predicament in which Barnabas found himself in Antioch. So many people were coming to faith in Christ that he couldn't keep up with the task of discipling them: "Then Barnabas went to Tarsus to look for Saul, and when he found him, he brought him to Antioch. So for a whole year Barnabas and Saul met with the church and taught great numbers of people" (Acts 11:25–26).

Barnabas treated Saul like an equal. They teamed up to teach God's word to the new believers. They also teamed up to travel together and plant churches (Acts 11:27–30; 13:1–14:28). And Saul (or Paul, as he was later called) replicated the process he had learned from Barnabas. When Paul came to Lystra, he spotted a young man named Timothy who had leadership potential (Acts 16:1–4). His instinct was to involve him in mission and ministry, just as Barnabas had included Paul in his partnership in the gospel.

One of the best ways to develop leaders with a shepherd heart is to train them to become small group leaders who in turn become trainers of other small group leaders. Church growth consultant and leadership development coach Carl George gives helpful advice on how to recruit a leader-in-training:

1. Commit yourself to being a leader who produces other group leaders.
2. Recruit apprentices who are willing to serve as leaders-in-training.
3. Use spiritual gift identification to draw untapped talent into leadership training roles.
4. Train your apprentice through modeling and feedback.
5. Make sure your apprentice has access to training beyond what you can provide.

Carl George says that the process of leadership training looks like this:

- I do, you watch, we talk.
- I do, you help, we talk.
- You do, I help, we talk.
- You do, I watch, we talk.
- We each begin to train someone else.[26]

I'm convinced that if we adopted Carl George's strategy, not just in our small groups, but also in every leadership role in the church, our churches would end up with an abundance of godly leaders. As we engage in a constant talent search for leaders-in-training, exemplify godly leadership, pass on information and skills that will empower them, and come alongside them as a coach, leaders as "trainers of leaders" will emerge. A mentor as coach affirms, "I want to provide opportunities for you to lead and to train others to lead."

5. Release: A Mentor as Team Player

IDENTIFICATION	IMITATION	INSTRUCTION	INVOLVEMENT	RELEASE
Talent Scout	Example	Teacher	Coach	Team Player

Rowland: My first experience of intentional leadership training was with a man from a parachurch ministry. He approached me when I was teaching school in Auckland, New Zealand, and asked if I would like to meet him for prayer and Bible study each Monday morning at 6:00 a.m. at the Harbor Bridge. It was a forty-five-minute drive from my home to the bridge, and I was expected to have had my daily appointment with God for at least forty-five minutes and learn a minimum of two Bible verses a week.

The relationship started well. I was blown away that someone would be willing to spend time praying with me and encouraging me. But then my mentor became very possessive. I felt as though I couldn't get out of the relationship. From that experience I learned several lessons. First, beware of anyone who talks about "my disciple" or "my protégé." Second, be open to times of intensive learning, but let the relationship be more fluid than possessive. Third, adopt a team approach to mentoring.

Luke records the incredibly productive mentoring relationship between Barnabas and Paul in Acts 11–15. Then we come to a sad chapter in their friendship—a major disagreement that led to a parting of the ways. Interestingly, Luke doesn't blame either party. He simply points out that the split in their peer-mentoring partnership resulted in two missionary teams being formed: Barnabas took John Mark and sailed for Cyprus, and Paul teamed up with Silas to strengthen the churches in Syria and Cilicia (Acts 15:39–40).

Adopting a team approach to mentoring is an effective way to overcome the tendency for mentoring relationships to become possessive. As a team of church leaders, look together at the five rings of mentoring identified in this chapter. Be open about the ways each of you can contribute to the development of the potential and emerging leaders you have identified. A mentor as team player conveys, "I'm here for you, not to control you, but to facilitate your growth as a leader. I'm mentoring with an open hand."

These five mentoring rings—identification, imitation, instruction, involvement, and release—are foundational elements in the equipping of servant-leaders in your church.

CHURCH-BASED MENTORING

What would a church-based strategy of mentoring leaders look like?

HOLD THE VALUE HIGH

For mentoring to become ingrained in your leadership development culture, you must hold the value high. The most important way to do this is for current leaders to model what it means to be a mentor. Ask yourself: Should having a mentor and being a mentor be included in the job descriptions of those in primary leadership roles in your church—pastors, elders, and ministry leaders?

If mentoring leaders is a high value in your church, it will be talked about frequently—in sermons, in classes, and in the testimonials of people whose lives have been transformed through intentional spiritual friendships. Less obvious, but just as important, is the appointment of a mentoring champion—someone who will ensure that mentoring is not just a lofty goal but a daily reality.

Don't Force It

I've heard it said that each leader should have a Paul, a Barnabas, and a Timothy—a mentor to look up to (a Paul), a peer-mentor (a Barnabas), and a protégé (a younger, less mature Timothy). When these three aspects of mentoring become a duty, a cast-iron requirement, the dimension of spiritual friendship is lost. It's better to say that each leader should recognize the need for a spiritual father/mother, a trusted peer, and an understudy.

Another common mistake is to try to force mentors and protégés together. Matching works fine for teaching ministry skills. A close relationship isn't necessary for learning how to conduct a wedding or funeral. Pairing people is much less likely to work, however, when it comes to character development. Rather than pairing people up, we can make available lists of people who are open to character-development mentoring relationships. Prospective mentors and protégés can be encouraged to get together to explore whether there is sufficient respect to continue. We can also conduct leadership courses for wisdom development, and from those groups we can encourage mentor pairs to emerge.

A TRIBUTE

Rowland: One of my mentors was my uncle, Dr. Will T. Miller, who took a personal interest in my career. In his letters he would tell me to attempt great things for God. He was the epitome of affirmation. As I think back on his life and his mentoring style (he's now with the Lord), what impresses me is that he was always there for me in those times when I needed his wisdom.

When our son Craig died at five months of age, Will and my aunt visited us and had the insight to know that we needed their presence more than their advice. When I was facing a major career change, my uncle appeared at exactly the right moment and gave affirmation and shared seasoned wisdom from the Bible. Sometimes he directed me; other times he coached me. Always he believed in me. I can't remember the car he drove, and the memories of the houses he lived in are fading, but his thumbprints are all over my life. The world is a better place because Uncle Will lived for the next generation.

To Consider and Discuss

1. What is mentoring? How is the term used in this chapter?

2. Have you ever experienced a mentoring relationship as a mentor or as a protégé? If so, describe one of your mentoring experiences.

3. How have you identified leaders in your ministry experience? Take some time to go through your church directory and identify potential leaders, emerging leaders, and existing leaders.

4. Why is imitation so powerful? How have you experienced the power of an imitative model in another person?

5. What kinds of instruction can you provide as a mentor?

6. In what ways are you involving developing leaders in real-life ministry?

7. What positive and negative experiences have you had (or observed) with "releasing"?

8. What would an overall leadership development strategy look like where courses, community, and mentoring are effectively interrelated?

Part Three

IMPLEMENTATION: FROM STRATEGY TO ACTION

GETTING STARTED

7

The goal of church-based training is "developing all believers to maturity and many to leadership in the local church, under the authority of local church leadership, with other churches, through an apprenticeship, on-the-job approach, for Christ's mission of multiplying churches worldwide." So if this is the goal, how do we get there? How do we implement church-based training in our own churches?

There is no one-size-fits-all answer to this question, but the following inventory walks through a sequence of steps many churches have found useful to organize their efforts and to make sure they're not overlooking a critical part of the process. This inventory is most valuable when used by a planning team rather than just by an individual. Feel free to make copies of this inventory for all team members.

117

CHURCH-BASED TRAINING IMPLEMENTATION INVENTORY

1. Start from biblical convictions.

Before you can lead people to focus on leadership development, you must first be convinced yourself. As you consider all the various church ministries, as well as all your responsibilities, what are your convictions about the relative value and importance of leadership development?

Inventory: How strong are your personal convictions about church-based training?

No convictions				Some convictions				Solid convictions	
1	2	3	4	5	6	7	8	9	10

It doesn't take long to circle a number from 1 to 10. It takes longer to move from evaluation to action. Before going on to the next step, make a plan and jot down some of your convictions.

Plan: I will schedule the following block of time to prayerfully study leadership development in God's Word: _____

_____

I already have the following convictions about developing leaders: (In a team setting, have each person share a personal conviction. This can be an inspirational moment.)

_____

_____

_____

_____

_____

_____

_____

_____

_____

_____

2. Design a development plan for bringing many into leadership.

Church-based training is more than simply an add-on program you try this semester. It is a fundamental value like "reaching the lost." Church-based training requires thinking holistically about the entire church ministry. Rather than just trying out a course, begin by developing an overall plan for how you'll accomplish this mission. A comprehensive plan (see chapter 3) will include courses, mentoring, and community for your board, staff, and emerging leaders, and it will be designed to develop leaders' heads, hearts, and hands.

Inventory: How far along is your church in the process of developing a church-based leadership development plan?

No plan				Some plan				Comprehensive plan	
1	2	3	4	5	6	7	8	9	10

Compare your numerical ranking with others on your planning team. In our seminars it's fascinating—and sometimes a bit tense—when fellow church leaders discover their evaluations either converging or diverging. Don't stop with evaluation, but begin now to compile your next steps in developing a leadership development plan.

Plan: I will take these next steps with these people to develop a church-based leadership development plan: _____

_____

_____

_____

_____

Briefly stated, this is our vision for developing leaders: (Another great team exercise is to have different leaders share their vision.)

_____

_____

_____

_____

_____

3. Build ownership and secure involvement by leaders.

One common mistake is to launch a program without ownership by the core leaders. This almost always leads to problems and sometimes even crises. Therefore, a critical step in implementing church-based training is to build ownership and secure involvement by key church leaders. This includes board and staff members, but it may also include financial givers, long-term members, and well-respected voices in the church. The most effective way to build ownership is not by "selling" your leaders on a program you've already designed, but rather by inviting them to share in designing your leadership development process. People invariably feel ownership of what they create.

How much ownership do core leaders have of your leadership development vision? A good indicator is how many of your core leaders are committed to being personally involved in leadership development.

> **Inventory:** What level of ownership and involvement do you observe in your core leaders (governing board members, staff members, and the like)?

None				Some					Total
1	2	3	4	5	6	7	8	9	10

If your score is below 8, it's time to get really practical. Name names. Who are the people whose ownership is critical to the effectiveness of church-based training in your church? Write down names of people you need to speak with. Intentionally develop steps you will take to encourage these people to become personally involved in leadership development. In one CCBT seminar, a church leader suggested inviting the senior pastor to attend a church-based training study group already in progress, and then asking the participants to share what the study meant to them. Other participants recommended a variety of actions: sending emails to key leaders in the church that tell of the impact the CCBT seminar made on them, inviting other leaders to a church-based training conference, reading a pertinent book together, holding several long and honest conversations on the topic, and going through a course with just the core leaders. These are all great ideas. Some way, somehow, you will need to interact personally with key leaders to encourage their ownership and involvement.

Plan: These are the people I consider key leaders whose ownership and involvement are needed: _____

_____

_____

_____

_____

_____

_____

I will take the following steps to encourage their ownership and involvement: _____

_____

_____

_____

_____

_____

_____

My first step and most strategic step is to _____

_____

_____

_____

_____

4. Assess your church's openness to change.

How receptive or resistant is your church to change? The last thing you want to do is tear your church apart by forcing change at such a rate that you rip the relational ties that hold your fellowship together. When convicted about a change a leader believes the church should make, frequently he or she wants to make the change immediately. Seasoned leaders, however, realize that wisdom calls us to pace change at a rate appropriate for our particular congregation at this point in its life. For maximum discernment, this kind of assessment is best made by a team of people.

Inventory: Rate your church's openness to change.

Resistant to change				Willing to change				Embraces change	
1	2	3	4	5	6	7	8	9	10

Plan: I will meet with the following persons or group to assess our church's current openness to change: _____

_____

_____

_____

_____

_____

We will meet on the following date: _____

5. Appoint a point person.

When a football team scores a touchdown, a player carries the ball over the goal line. If you want to see church-based training effectively implemented in your church, then someone needs to carry the ball. This can be a paid staff member, a board member, or a key volunteer. When it is *everyone's* job, it is no one's job—and nothing happens.

Think about the leaders at your church. Who do you think would be a good candidate to serve as your point person for church-based training?

Inventory: Rate your "point person" options.

No one available				A few possibilities				Have the right person	
1	2	3	4	5	6	7	8	9	10

Plan: I will pray about this short list of people who may be equipped to serve as our point person. Circle the name you believe is your best person to serve in this role.

_____

_____

_____

_____

_____

_____

6. Decide on a launch strategy.

We've seen four basic strategies emerge as the most common ways of launching church-based training: Skunk Works,[27] existing group, emerging leaders, and core leaders.

Skunk Works: A "Skunk Works" approach envisions trying out a course or two in a specific ministry before going churchwide with the materials. This approach can work well in a large church where you can experiment in a singles' group or a men's or women's ministry. However, even if it goes well, you run the risk of getting underway without the full participation and ownership of your core leaders.

Existing Group: Another approach is to work with an existing group, such as a Sunday school class or a small group, that currently uses some other curriculum. This will occasionally work, but it often doesn't because your visionary message—your paradigm change—can get undercut in a simplistic debate about which study material group members liked best. Most people prefer dessert (hot topics) to the meat and potatoes (core issues).

Emerging Leaders: Many churches have a group of young up-and-coming leaders who are eager to grow. They are the church leaders of the future who are probably already serving in various roles today, but not on the board or staff. These folks usually love to take any new course that's offered, consuming everything you can give them. The danger is that, infused with fresh knowledge and vision, they will challenge the existing leaders. Untempered by maturity, sometimes these challenges can lead to major crises and even church splits.

Core Leaders: For most churches, we recommend launching church-based training with your core leaders. If you start with your most respected leaders, the rest of the body will want to follow them. If people start hearing about "this great study" that the board or pastors are involved in, they'll tend to ask, "Can we do it too?" The following semester you can then offer the course to the church as a whole, touting it as the one the leadership group has done. Starting with core leaders also ensures their active involvement and solicits their ownership. They will understand and embrace the vision more deeply because they have experienced it.

Your core leadership most likely includes three groups—board members, staff pastors, and key volunteer leaders. One of these three may well be your best group with which to begin. As a general rule, you should start with the group that has the greatest influence. In some churches, you may want to combine two groups. For example, in a church with one or two associate pastors, the associate pastor(s) might join the church board for the study. In a church of fifty with an elder board of three people, you might want to include key volunteers in the study group.

Inventory: How open are your board members, staff members, and key volunteers to church-based leadership development? (You may want to rate each group differently.)

No groups open   One group open   All three groups open

1	2	3	4	5	6	7	8	9	10

Plan: If we implement church-based leadership development in our church, we will most likely start with (pick one or more groups):

_____

_____

_____

_____

7. Choose a curriculum.

While principles and process are more important than the particular tool you use, the tool is also important. You will want to find the best available resources to help you develop people into leaders.

Inventory: Rate your available curricular tools to develop leaders.

No tool   Used some tools   Love our tool

1	2	3	4	5	6	7	8	9	10

Plan: I will take this step (or these steps) to help our church select a good tool to be used for developing leaders: _____

_____

_____

_____

_____

_____

8. Assign resources.

All ministries take money, space, and time. How you allocate your budget, your facilities, and your calendar will reveal the degree to which you value leadership development.

Money: How much of your church budget is directed toward leadership development? When is your next budget cycle? How much money will it take to do church-based training well? What will you charge for church-based training events? Will you provide food?

Space: Where in the building will you hold classes? In the corner room in the basement with poor lighting and water seeping through the wall, or in the bright, warm room by the kitchen?

Time: When will your training be? Monday morning at 6:00 a.m., or prime-time Sunday evening at 6:00 p.m.? Every church ministry wants to be fully funded and meet in the best room at the best time—which is impossible, so we must make choices and set priorities.

Inventory: What kind of priority does your church place on its allocation of resources for developing leaders?

No priority   Moderate priority   High priority

| 1 | 2 | 3 | 4 | 5 | 6 | 7 | 8 | 9 | 10 |

Plan: I will take this step (or these steps) to help our church give a high priority to developing leaders as expressed in how we assign our resources:

Money: _____

_____

_____

Space: _____

_____

_____

_____

Time: _____

_____

_____

9. Set an implementation timeline.

When are you going to take specific steps to build ownership among core leaders, develop your plan, and cast the vision? How long will it take? When do you want to start your first training course, and with whom? Backing up from that date, when will you need to recruit the participants and order materials?

Inventory: How complete is your church's implementation timeline?

No timeline   Partial timeline   Complete timeline

| 1 | 2 | 3 | 4 | 5 | 6 | 7 | 8 | 9 | 10 |

Plan: I will develop a timeline with the appropriate people by this date:

_____

_____

10. Communicate the new vision, values, and strategic plan.

You must communicate with the entire church family so they catch the vision and embrace the plan. Use multiple means of communication: sermons, letters, phone calls, emails, meetings, drama skits, posters, your website, newsletters. It's almost impossible to overcommunicate. Invariably someone will still say, "I never heard about it."

Inventory: Rate your communication of your vision, values, and plan.

Little communication   Some communication   Saturation communication

| 1 | 2 | 3 | 4 | 5 | 6 | 7 | 8 | 9 | 10 |

Plan: I will communicate the new vision for developing leaders in these ways:

_____

_____

_____

_____

_____

_____

_____

11. Recruit your first group of participants.

Which people do you want in your first group(s)? Identify each person by name. Create in advance a potential roster and make a personal contact with each person, inviting him or her to the training event or course.

Inventory: How far along are you in lining up your first group of participants?

No participants   A few possible   All recruited

1	2	3	4	5	6	7	8	9	10

Plan: I will recruit these people as my first target participants:

_____

_____

_____

_____

_____

_____

_____

_____

12. Grow the training.

Once you get underway, you will face the challenges of retention, ongoing training, and extending the training to even more people.

Retention: Even when people are eager for an initial training experience, it's not uncommon to see them drop out before a second course begins. After you've recruited people, you'll need to continually motivate them to stay with it. Help people see the benefit. Plan breaks between sessions— but not for too long a period, or people will fill their time with other activities.

Ongoing training: The facilitators who lead your courses are your most strategic people. If you have a poor facilitator, you will have a lousy class. A good facilitator will enable almost any group with any curriculum to have a good learning experience. Offer training for your facilitators before every new semester. In addition, your point person should provide coaching and encouragement to all your facilitators on a weekly basis.

Extend the training throughout the church: If your first group is successful, you'll want to expand to an increasing number of people. Soon you'll face the issue of how to extend your model for leadership development throughout the whole church. How you intend to handle this training extension issue should be part of your comprehensive plan. No matter what size your church is, it is challenging to orient all the leaders and ministries around a common vision, yet it is crucial to your health and to kingdom impact.

Help other churches: Finally, if God allows you a measure of success in seeing people develop as leaders in your local body, you may have an opportunity to help other churches. We dream of a global network of churches that are passionate to assist other churches in their spheres of influence to implement church-based training.

Inventory: What steps have you taken to grow your training?

No steps				A few steps				Solid plan in place	
1	2	3	4	5	6	7	8	9	10

Plan: What steps will you take to:

retain people in training? _____

_____

_____

train your facilitators? _____

_____

_____

extend your training to new groups? _____

_____

_____

help other churches? _____

_____

_____

PITFALLS TO AVOID

Here are some fairly common pitfalls you'll want to avoid:

1. *Lack of ownership at the start.* It is critical that your key leaders share the vision before you launch church-based leadership development. If they don't, you are setting the stage for conflict.
2. *Insecurity caused by speed of change.* Any change is disruptive, so start slowly and give people time to adjust. It is better to go slowly and succeed than to go quickly and risk things blowing up in your face.
3. *Divisions in the church.* A church divided is a danger, especially when you choose to bypass your key leaders and start with a development group on the side. As subleaders learn more about the vision for developing all believers to maturity and many to leadership, they can easily become critical of those who haven't had the same opportunity to be exposed to the training.
4. *Time pressure on the pastor.* It will not work simply to add the task of training leaders to a pastor's already overflowing job description. For any pastor who is ready to invest significant time in leadership development, something else will have to give. Your church may have to hire additional support staff (office or facility) or equipping staff, or perhaps your pastor will have to decide to stop doing some less important tasks.
5. *Disruption due to pastoral transition.* Church-based training should not be launched just before a change in senior pastors takes place. Give time throughout the transition for the church leaders to embrace the process so it can thrive through a pastoral changeover.
6. *Elitism.* Some trainees may develop an elitist mentality. Treat this as a serious character issue, and don't allow it to continue unchecked. Be sure you have a plan in place to offer

a clear pathway for everyone else in the church to grow as leaders.

7. *Training for training's sake.* We can easily fall in love with learning and lose sight of the church's mission. We are training leaders in order to reach out to the lost, to spread the gospel by multiplying churches locally and worldwide.

If you've come to this point in the chapter and have simply read the material, consider following this good first step with a second: Set aside some time to work through the "Implementation Inventory" for your own church, preferably with a planning team.

YOUR CHURCH-BASED TRAINING ACTION PLAN

Here's a summary of the sequence of steps your church can take as it begins to consider the vision of church-based training and its implementation at the grassroots level:

- Start from biblical convictions.
- Design a development plan for bringing many into leadership.
- Build ownership and secure involvement by leaders.
- Assess your church's openness to change.
- Appoint a point person.
- Decide on a launch strategy.
- Choose a curriculum.
- Assign resources.
- Set an implementation timeline.
- Communicate the new vision, values, and strategic plan.
- Recruit your first group of participants.
- Grow the training.

To Consider and Discuss

1. What are the benefits of working through the "Implementation Inventory" with a team?

2. What question in the inventory presents the greatest challenge to your church? Why?

3. Why is it crucial to assess your church's openness to change?

4. Where are you in the process of implementation as a church?

5. What part of the implementation timeline requires your attention right now?

6. What pitfalls do you need to be especially careful of in your church?

EQUIPPING YOUR GOVERNING BOARD

8

After being elected to his church board, Tim was surprised to find out that he would receive no training for his new role. He had gone through intensive training to serve as a small group leader, and he was expected to go through additional training from time to time to improve his ministry skills in that area. When he had joined his church's greeting team, he had received training. It didn't make sense to Tim that he would be trained for these ministries but not for his ministry as a church board member.

He asked several other board members what their responsibilities were and was disconcerted by their often conflicting responses. Some were indifferent about their role, others uncertain and insecure, and a few even seemed preoccupied with the power and status of their position. Tim was thankful that most members of the congregation were unaware of this sad condition of the elder board, and he stepped into his new role determined to make the most of a difficult situation.

Although Tim was surprised by what he found, this state of affairs is all too familiar to most pastors. Church board members are typically people of proven faithfulness who possess leadership skills. Yet, few receive more than a brief orientation for this ministry that is so critical to the effectiveness of the church.

A significant gap of theological knowledge and practical experience exists between many pastors and their governing boards. Most pastors have had extensive training for ministry—formal theological training and opportunities to learn from their peers and to participate in seminars and conferences. This lack of parity in training can sometimes cause friction between board members and full-time pastors. If unattended, the gap can widen as the pastoral staff grows in ministry training and experience while the board members remain relative novices in their understanding of crucial aspects of church leadership.

The Ephesians 4 job description of pastors includes equipping God's people for works of service. A key responsibility of a pastor is to spearhead efforts to equip board members to be effective in their roles as church leaders.

The book of Acts tells us of a leadership crisis that arose in the church in Jerusalem. The apostles had gotten so busy serving people's physical needs that they couldn't place enough focus on "prayer and the ministry of the word" (Acts 6:4). They solved the problem by appointing seven others to lead the ministry to widows, which freed them to focus on their primary role.

If your church leaders are distracted from prayer and study of God's Word, then they have a problem. If your leaders aren't devoted to regularly evaluating your church in light of the ideals of God's Word, they are missing a key aspect of their role.

Jeff and Bruce: At Fellowship we began to recognize in 1989 that our elders were not as effective as they needed to be. Their duties were essentially limited to evaluating and approving proposals from the pastoral staff. They were paying attention mostly to the administrative details of such matters as facilities and staff benefits. They were not devoted to prayer and God's Word in any meaningful way. We addressed the situation by creating a management team that would focus on the administrative aspects of our church, which freed the elders to concentrate on more important tasks. We designed an ongoing training process shaped by the question, "What do all church board members need to know, be, and do in order to fulfill their responsibilities?" Much of what we learned is now included in a series of courses produced by the Center for Church Based Training (www.ccbt.org).

PRACTICAL BENEFITS
OF TRAINING YOUR BOARD MEMBERS

Our board members have greatly appreciated the time we invest in their training. As their confidence has grown, their impact and effectiveness as church leaders has also grown. Since receiving this training, most of them have traveled internationally to train pastors and other key church leaders. We have seen the strong correlation between the health of the church and the degree to which our key leaders are grounded in such basics as the nature and function of the church; the character, function, and skills of a godly leader; and the mission of the organization they are leading. And this grounding, in our experience, comes largely through effective, ongoing training!

GREATER UNITY

Jeff: I once served in a church with a dysfunctional, untrained board. Board members were often at odds with pastors and each other. Meetings scheduled to last two hours would on occasion extend into the early hours of the next day. Decisions that should have been made in minutes often took weeks. You can imagine the tension and hurt feelings! The church was immobilized by the board's dysfunction.

At Fellowship, our training process has produced board unity on foundational issues of church life and leadership. As part of their training, our board members engage in deep discussions about the church's overall vision and direction. They compare the ideal biblical picture of the church with the church's present reality. From this emerging vision of what the church could be, they develop strategies that correspond with this vision. Our elders love these discussions because they are talking about "real issues," not merely what color of carpet to buy for the nursery. Imagine board consensus on such hot topics as worship and music, the role of the church in politics and culture, church discipline, church mission, and financial priorities.

This process of constantly comparing present reality to the biblical ideal keeps us from getting locked into ministry forms that are no longer effective. Our board is constantly reinventing the way we do church so we can stay effective over the long haul.

We often hear positive comments about the unity of our leadership team. We believe we owe much of the unity we experience to the time we spend together in prayer and God's Word (Acts 6:4). You may find that the most significant change in your church happens when you begin to equip your board and discuss key issues proactively.

SHARED VISION

Lately a number of writers have proposed a model of vision crafting in which the pastor "hears" from God a vision for the church and then presents it to the leadership team to adopt and implement. We believe this model of unilateral leadership is flawed. Our experience has confirmed that a collaborative approach in which key leaders work together as a team will deliver better results. The pastor may be facilitating and leading the process, but the whole team is involved from the beginning. This can make the difference between a pastor's merely getting permission from the board and the board's taking full ownership. A vision deeply shared by the leadership team will have far greater impact than one to which they're merely consenting.

What emerges from the process is not just one person's vision but a vision that taps into the collective wisdom of the group in a way that helps preserve doctrinal and philosophical integrity. While adaptations to this collaborative approach may be called for if the board is too large or dispersed to achieve in-depth discussion, a team approach should be foundational to vision crafting.

Less Lobbying

Another value of training for board members lies in what pastor and leadership speaker Larry Osborne describes as the distinction between training and lobbying.[28] He defines training as presenting information away from the pressure and need to make an immediate decision. Training changes *the way people think.* He defines lobbying as presenting information in the middle of the decision-making process. Lobbying is designed to change *the way people vote.* Church board members tend to resist lobbying because they are skeptical about whether the information is objective and balanced. A pastor may, for instance, introduce a "study process" concurrent with his or her push to build a larger facility. The board is asked to study various articles written by church growth experts who make the case that great churches emphasize adequate parking, children's and youth facilities, and state-of-the-art worship centers. Whether or not the pastor is trying to manipulate the board's decisions, it can sometimes feel that way.

Churches that provide ongoing training for their key leaders are often receptive to change when stretching decisions need to be made. When training is part of the church leadership culture, board members have time to adjust their thinking, change their paradigm, and develop well-informed opinions apart from the pressure of an urgent decision.

Jeff: Here's an example of how this can work. For over twenty-five years, Fellowship has been part of a church-planting movement that has spawned about three hundred Fellowship-type churches across the United States and beyond. Dr. Gene Getz spearheaded this effort for years by emphasizing to his church leaders the biblical mission of multiplying churches. So when he introduced a proposal to plant a new church fifteen miles away, the board offered immediate support, even though it meant investing a lot of money and inviting a number of church members to join the effort. A lobbying push, even by a strong founding pastor, would not have produced the same result. In our case, the elders not only vigorously supported the project but also generously expanded the initial proposal. The continued growth of both Fellowship and the new church is a powerful testimony to God's blessing on the process.

KEYS TO EFFECTIVE CHURCH-BASED BOARD TRAINING

Not just any training program will produce these results of greater unity, shared vision, and less lobbying. Here are ten keys to shaping a training process that can help yield these results:

1. COMMIT TO REGULAR, ONGOING TRAINING

Jeff and Bruce: At Fellowship the elders wouldn't have experienced these benefits without regular training over a period of years. The extended time together allows us to discuss crucial issues without feeling pressured by the need to make a decision. In addition, significant decisions and initiatives we couldn't have anticipated have often grown out of our discussions, as iron sharpened iron (see Proverbs 27:17).

We have found that it works best for the board to meet either every other week or weekly for a semester and then take a break. Monthly sessions make it hard to maintain a sense of connection and continuity.

2. TAKE TIME TO BUILD RELATIONSHIPS

Use the training time to strengthen the bonds among leadership team members. Allow them to share their concerns and to pray for each other and for the church. This is a prime opportunity for pastors to shepherd their boards. Make your training an opportunity for spiritual and emotional renewal.

Jeff: Currently at Fellowship we reserve the first thirty minutes for prayer requests, updates, and prayers for each other and about any major church concerns. We often end our discussion time with extended prayer about the central topic. In a recent session about church discipline, for example, we set aside considerable time to pray that our church leaders would lead holy lives and would finish strong.

3. Separate Your Study Time from Your Business Meeting

Strive to keep business discussions in business meetings and to do your training another time. Tacking on ten to twenty minutes of training at the beginning of a business meeting is seldom effective. Most board members will see this time as a prelude to the real meeting, and their minds will drift until business discussions begin, or you'll find that the business issues will crowd out the training time.

Generating productive discussion takes time—often too much time to add as an agenda item to a typical board meeting. We've found that a ninety-minute discussion is about what it takes to produce the kind of interaction that works to unify the board, delve deeply into important issues, and promote lasting change— and it's also about the limit of a person's ability to concentrate on any particular discussion.

Expect some initial passive—maybe even active—resistance to the idea of regular, ongoing meetings. Active resistors may say, "Do we have to do one more meeting?" Passive resistors may say what you want to hear, but they just won't show up at the meetings. You'll have to communicate the benefits of the process, then make sure that your discussions really do add value. Take the time to prepare well so that you don't waste your board's time.

Regardless of how you position it, your training discussions may feel like a second-tier meeting to the business meeting. However, over time, if you do your job well, board members will come to regard the church-based training sessions as their most strategic gathering.

4. Find the Most Helpful Venue for Your Church-Based Training Discussions

Jeff: Location greatly affects the tone of your meetings. We've found that meetings held in our church office facility to be somewhat impersonal, inhibited, and closure oriented—and sometimes an environment that generates significant dissent. We prefer to meet in homes because we've found that in a home setting, people are more relaxed, more open, and more personal. Our discussions are not mere intellectual exercises, but they include very personal and, at times, even highly emotional discussions.

Food enhances the atmosphere. While the homes and neighborhoods in which we meet often shine the spotlight on differences, most of us eat and enjoy food. Eating together seems to de-emphasize our differences and promote camaraderie. God himself associates close fellowship with him with food in Israel's feast days, the sacrament of the Lord's Supper, his overture to the church in Laodicea to let him come in and eat with them, and the wedding supper of the Lamb.[29] After the resurrection, the immortal Christ, needing no food to live, prepared a breakfast of broiled fish for his disciples (John 21:9–13). His overarching purpose was to build a sense of connection, not to fill hungry stomachs.

5. Expect Regular Attendance; Update Any Members Who Are Absent

If you've done your job well, the interest and commitment of your board members will increase. But your good work can be undermined by members who, for whatever reason, are lax about their attendance. When board members miss meetings, they may feel guilty about reengaging the process. Work hard to find a time to meet that will enable every board member to attend the leadership development sessions regularly. Then ask them to make a strong commitment to attend. On those occasions when members must miss sessions, be sure to provide them with timely, detailed updates. Doing so will enable them to stay current on important issues and to feel confident about contributing to future discussions.

6. Focus on the Big Picture: Training Is More about Shaping the Church Than about Personal Development

Remind board members regularly of how relevant their efforts are to the effectiveness of the church. Momentum will slide if leaders think that training is only about *personal* development. God will hold us accountable as leaders for the direction and health of our churches. We are responsible for how we respond to new ideas and information. Our efforts should make a measurable difference in the quality of our churches.

7. Use Study Materials Designed to Stimulate Board Interaction

Using prepared materials has several advantages. First, you don't have to reinvent the wheel. It takes far less time to adapt existing resources to your setting than to create your own study materials. Second, courses produced by another organization can give your training process more credibility. Third, using outside resources can shield you from criticism from any who may otherwise wonder if you're introducing personal biases into the process in order to promote a private agenda.

We suggest great flexibility in your use of printed resources. Sometimes you'll hit on a lesson topic that, given your particular situation, demands more than a single session. You may need to add a topic not covered by your basic curriculum. Or you may decide to skip a session that won't be helpful in your unique setting.

Jeff: Our pastoral team and board recently studied "Church Dynamics," a course developed by the Center for Church Based Training. As we discussed the relationship between the church and the surrounding culture, we felt the need to spend more time identifying the basic principles that would govern our approach to various social and political issues. The two additional months we spent collaborating in study and discussions resulted in a well-developed position paper that we can give to those who ask about the basis of our involvement in social and cultural events and activities.

8. Coordinate Board Training with Pastoral Staff Training

In a church with more than one pastor on staff, it's important that you either include the other pastors in the board training times or that you provide concurrent training for your pastors. To keep your leaders "singing out of the same hymnbook," both groups need to be grappling with the same issues. For pastors to be truly excited about board initiatives that may emerge from participation in a training course, they need to be part of the process.

Jeff: At Fellowship, the material we cover in board training sessions parallels what the pastors are covering. Our pastoral staff is too large to meet regularly with the board, so a couple of our pastors attend board meetings to make sure our efforts are coordinated. These pastors keep each group up-to-date with the other group's discussions. Doing so has produced a synergistic relationship between our pastors and board members in which those who normally implement necessary changes—the pastors—participate in key discussions throughout the process, which in turn eliminates unnecessary surprises and promotes consensus.

9. Include Spouses Whenever Possible

Church-based training discussions tend to be deeper and more transformational when spouses participate. What's more, when you include them in the meeting, it means you're not asking your elders to leave their spouses for yet another meeting.

10. Develop an Entry Process for New Elders

Jeff: When new elders come into the group, we try to enfold them—two couples at a time. My wife and I meet with the two couples for a couple of months and accompany them through a self- and group-evaluation period before they officially adopt the role of elder. We typically read through *The Measure of a Man* by Gene Getz, which reviews the basic character qualities essential for eldership.[30] At the end of the book is a diagnostic inventory that prospective elders complete. They then ask several fellow leaders who know them well to rate them, using the same inventory. This process has at times flagged character issues that prompted elder candidates to delay their appointment as elders to work on problem areas. In the case of one of our elders, we held the position open for a couple of years until both he and others were satisfied that he was biblically qualified to serve as an elder.

As a second step, some of our sitting elders facilitate an out-of-town retreat focused on bringing clarity to the roles and responsibilities of being an elder. I like to combine the discussions with some physical challenges geared to deepening relationships and getting a glimpse at how each person may function on the team. Over the last couple of years, we've taken prospective elders to the Texas desert in the Big Bend area, staging some rigorous hikes in the rugged desert. You can learn a lot about someone in that kind of environment.

Once elders begin their new role, my wife and I continue to meet with the new couples for several months, going over some of the more significant issues the existing elders have discussed. It catches them up with the rest of the group and ensures continuity with both the philosophy and direction of our ministry.

CONCLUSION

Developing and unifying your board is one of the best possible investments of a pastor's time. A church-based training effort geared to helping prepare and strengthen board members can make serving on the board a rich experience. The relational bonds that develop in the process make the job fun—as it should be. Most important, though, board members enjoy the reward of seeing the fruit their work bears through a healthier, more effective church.

To Consider and Discuss

1. How would you characterize the level of training given to the governing board at your church?

2. Do you see a gap between the board and the pastoral staff? Why or why not? If you perceive a gap, how would you describe it?

3. What obstacles might a church board encounter in attempting to do leadership development together?

4. How does the responsibility that the board shoulders infuse energy into the training?

5. What benefits can a board gain from being involved in leadership development? What benefits might your church gain?

6. What pattern of training do you think would work best for your church board?

EQUIPPING YOUR EMERGING LEADERS

9

Jeff: "Fourth quarter is ours! Fourth quarter is ours!" I can still remember hearing that cry as a boy at Alabama football games. In those years, Bear Bryant coached Alabama to be one of the dominant football teams in the country. In Alabama, he seemed to have as much clout as God and may have received more adoration.

He was a great coach, and key to his strategy was the depth of his bench. This was before the rulings by the NCAA that limited the number of players who could suit up for a game. The Alabama sidelines were virtually full from end zone to end zone with players in the wings and ready to go. They dwarfed most other teams by comparison.

Because of the strength of the bench, if we were behind at halftime or even into the third quarter, fans would hold up four fingers on one hand and shout, "Fourth quarter is ours!" Other teams would have worn out their first couple of strings by then, but we had an army of fresh players to put in the game. Alabama tended to dominate the fourth quarter because they had so many players ready to relieve the starters.

Good coaches work hard to develop player depth. They develop the second, third, and fourth strings so they don't wear out their starters. They know the power of a deep bench.

It's easy in ministry to run our "first string" ragged. The tendency to overwork the most willing and capable leaders seems to be universal, regardless of church size. Carl George makes this observation:

> The typical church involves about 10 percent of its people in public leadership. They usually constitute the talent pool for electable office or appointment—the highly visible places of congregational leadership.... The good news is that there is another undiscovered group that has not been tapped into because its "members" don't have the desire or need to put themselves forward.... They have the intelligence, character, heart, gifts, and ability to be effective leaders if invited to do so; but they usually won't offer themselves.... They are discovered leaders, not self-named leaders.[31]

BUILDING A DEEPER ROSTER

How do we develop "player depth" in our church? How do we spot emerging leaders and equip them to make vital contributions to the team's mission?

1. AN INTENTIONAL DISCIPLESHIP PROCESS

To multiply leaders for our church, we have to focus first on multiplying maturing disciples. The Center for Church Based Training has a slogan for this: "bringing all to maturity and many to leadership." We must have a process that grounds people in the faith and brings them to spiritual maturity. Not all of these people will become leaders, because God hasn't designed them for that role. Yet, you can't have mature leaders if you don't have spiritually mature people.

Imagine if you had an intentional discipleship process that produced an army of maturing believers from which many leaders could arise. At Fellowship, we have a two-year process called *Discovery*,[32] which is designed to deepen people in their faith. In an interactive small group process, they discuss with others the key issues of the Christian life. Their worldview and values begin to conform to biblical truth. They become motivated to build their lives around the glory and purpose of God expressed through the local church.

Before we had an intentional discipleship process, we really weren't sure what was happening in people's lives. Now, as people enter into *Discovery*, we confidently expect significant life-change. Around fifteen hundred of our people have gone through the *Discovery* process, and it has had a powerful impact on our church. Those who come out of *Discovery* are motivated to serve and spiritually equipped to lead—which has given us a huge pool of faithful servants and potential leaders.

2. A Leadership Pipeline

If you want to multiply leaders for your church, you should have a way to track people's progress. Though some at Fellowship think it's a cold, mechanistic term, we use the image of a *pipeline.* If you want leaders coming out, you have to have prospective leaders coming in. And you have to make sure that people keep moving through the pipeline and that you eliminate any bottlenecks.

Tracking the progress of emerging leaders is especially important if you choose to decentralize the function of identifying prospective leaders, as we suggested earlier—giving a baton to each leader. You need to know the following:

- Who have been identified as potential leaders?
- Where are they currently in their spiritual growth and ministry experience?
- Who is working with them?
- What next step can we encourage them to take?
- How far along are they?
- What are they passionate about, which then indicates where they're likely to be headed?

A good database-tracking program would be ideal for this, and it would be a great project for a computer programmer in your church to tackle. Fellowship still does this manually. We put names on magnetic strips on a large whiteboard in one of our conference rooms. It looks like a war room, but it works. We can look at the board and tell which people have been identified as prospective leaders, whether they've been invited to join our emerging leader's process, which people are working with them—and we can then discuss what next step we should invite each of them to consider.

By looking at the pipeline, we can see how we're doing at identifying and developing new leaders. If we need new small group leaders, for example, we can see which names are at the very end of the pipeline—those who are ready to take on the responsibility. And if we have only a few names at the front end of the pipeline, we know that down the road we're going to be leadership challenged if we don't begin soon to identify more prospective leaders.

3. AN I³ EMERGING LEADERS PROCESS

Why not challenge all of your existing leaders to be I³ leaders? The challenge is for them to commit to three I's: Identify, Invite, and Invest.

Identify

For your leaders to identify future leaders, you must let them know the qualities they should be looking for. Your list may include a certain level of character maturity, good innate leadership skills, and a teachable spirit. Your leaders should look for people who have the ability to attract a loyal following and who have influence within their group or ministry, even if they have recently joined the group or ministry. They should also look for a good fit between the potential leader and your church's vision and values.

Invite

Train your current leaders to invite others to consider entering an emerging leaders' process. This process can be formal or informal, but either way it is highly relational. The invitation should include a vision of how the potential leaders could enhance the work of the church. What in their lives suggests that they could be great leaders?

Prospective leaders also should know what they are being invited to. Don't promise too much, but also make sure that what you're inviting them to is substantial and worth their time. At this early stage, it might be a mentoring relationship, a training process at your church, or a particular responsibility for them to assume and cut their leadership teeth on.

Inviting people to leadership is one of our favorite things to do. Only rarely have people said no, and never has anybody been offended. People feel honored to be recognized and named as a person of potential. Why wouldn't they be?

Jeff: Sometimes we shrink back from inviting those with the greatest potential because they are already busy. Recently, a leader I invited to take on greater responsibility inspired me to keep on inviting good people without hesitation. Mike is a very busy person with strong leadership gifts. I was thanking him for saying yes and getting involved, and he said to me, "Jeff, I like you, and I would do a lot for you. But when you thank me like this, it's as if you think I'm doing this for you. I'm not. I'm just thrilled that I get to do this. My life has been changed and blessed because you asked me to come into this process and to take this responsibility. So I'm going to write out a thank-you note to you. You saw potential, and you asked. Thank you. And don't stop asking." How many people out there are like this? The more we can empower people to invite potential leaders to take the next step, the more contagious it will become.

Invest

Investing in emerging leaders requires coming alongside them by doing ministry together. Since life-on-life mentoring isn't a natural skill for most leaders, we have to train people to do it and support it with great tools. One tool we've used with good success is the Center for Church Based Training's *Life Development Planner*. This planner helps mentors build an individualized leadership development plan for potential leaders by clarifying their dreams and direction, as well as by identifying developmental gaps in their character, knowledge, and skills. Once the gaps are identified, the mentor and emerging leader can design a process for filling them in.

Rowland: Dan and I met each other through our mutual friendship with Jeff Jones. Our wives, Barbara and Elaine, quickly became close friends, while Dan and I proceeded more cautiously. We were members of Dan and Barbara's minichurch (small group) for a while. We supplemented our small group experience with meals and sailing trips together. Then Dan and I started meeting weekly for breakfast—initially not aiming to accomplish more than mutual encouragement and friendship.

In one way, it's a stretch to call Dan an emerging leader. When we met, he was a highly regarded small group leader. However, if you define "emerging leader" as "emerging elder," then the label fits. I've been a small cog in his development as an elder at Fellowship. In the period when Dan was being considered for eldership, I taught a "Life Development Planner" course he was taking. The participants work toward their "Life Development Plan," which contains their life-purpose statement, their divine design (including their gifts, interests, and passions), and their life-development timeline. They also identify gaps in their knowledge, character, and skills.

One week, over breakfast, Dan discussed his knowledge, character, and ministry skill goals. He had been asked to consider becoming an elder at Fellowship. I asked how I could help him in his development as an elder. His "Life Development Plan" had identified gaps in his knowledge of theology, so together we decided to add Wayne Grudem's *Bible Doctrine* to our breakfast of cereal and yogurt. Dan identified doctrines he wanted to study, and we made those chapters the main part of our discussion each week. What amazed me was the depth of fellowship we experienced as we wrestled with doctrines that will be helpful for him to grasp as he serves as one of the elder-shepherds in our church. I've learned as much from him as he has from me.

4. "LEADERSHIP UNIVERSITY"

At Fellowship in 2003, we had a nine-month "Leadership University" for training emerging leaders. Though available to all current leaders, it was open to potential leaders only by invitation. Thus, people saw it as a real privilege to be invited. The entry requirements included

- consistently engaging in worship, community, growth, service, and outreach (the five purposes of our church);
- exhibiting spiritual maturity and vitality;
- being respected by others;
- being excited about God's divine design for his or her life; and
- being on board with the Fellowship vision.

Those who accept an invitation to "Leadership University" make a nine-month commitment, entering with a "class" that goes through the process together. They experience community with the other emerging leaders, forming relationships that in some cases last for years. They participate in training modules taught by various pastors and leaders. They read books that help shape their theological understanding and philosophy of ministry. This has been a great training ground and confidence builder for our potential and existing leaders. It has also been a great way for them to get to know up close some of our pastors and key leaders.

"LEADERSHIP UNIVERSITY" SYLLABUS

☐ Life Development Plan		3 weeks
☐ The Bible (Bible study methods and survey)		4 weeks
☐ The Church (philosophy of church; evangelism and culture)		2 weeks
☐ Leadership		3 weeks
☐ Theology		6 weeks
☐ Elective		1 week

Reading:[33] *The Ascent of a Leader, Spiritual Disciples for the Christian Life,* and *Lost in America*

Consider how your church might design a similar training process for emerging leaders that reflects your own church's values, theology, and philosophy of ministry. Keep in mind that this is more than a class; it is a *learning community.* Essential to the experience are the relationships that form with fellow participants. Each leader has a mentor working alongside him or her in ministry during these nine months. "Leadership University" is not for everybody, but it has been an experience greatly appreciated by those who have graduated.

5. LEADERSHIP ORIENTATION

We host Leadership Orientation a couple of times a year for leaders who are ready to be commissioned to their new assignments. These orientations are always a highlight for me. It's the time when we give each leader a baton and talk about how they can identify, invite, and invest in the lives of other potential leaders. We want them to be on the lookout from the very beginning. Each leader also fills out a commitment form in which they promise to uphold our church's vision, values, and doctrine, and they vow to pursue unity in the church and purity in their own lives.

We also tell them what we are committing to them and what they can hold us accountable for as it relates to their ongoing encouragement, training, and support. We file these documents; at times we have to pull one out and go over it with a leader who is failing to uphold one of the commitments. These leaders then have the choice to recommit or to consider stepping down from leadership.

However you design it, a rite of passage for new leaders can give you one more opportunity to clarify your vision and inspire the new leaders who are entering your church ministries.

6. CHALLENGE NIGHTS

You'll often have emerging leaders who are "on the fence." They've been invited into leadership, but they need a little extra nudge. Some need a strong dose of vision to motivate them to give their time. Others need a strong dose of confidence. One way to encourage these people is to host a meeting (a dessert, for example) where the key visionary of your church or ministry shares the vision and invites people to leadership. Being able to rub shoulders with this visionary is inspiring to the emerging leaders, and that extra bit of vision casting and encouragement often helps people cross over the line to say yes to the invitation.

COACHING YOUR STARTING LINEUP

While we should do all we can to add depth to our team roster, it cannot be at the expense of our starting lineup. How do you continue to improve the skills of your starters—those, other than church staff, who are already active ministry leaders?

First, each ministry needs to provide training and encouragement for its own team members. Second, you need to offer high-quality training opportunities and vision nights for all your leaders. Involving your core leaders in these large group gatherings is a great way not only to equip them but also to honor them for their ministry.

We have suggested applying three key dynamics of leadership development—courses, community, and mentoring—to each group you seek to develop. What would it look like to do this with your existing leaders? As an example of how this can work, here is how Fellowship provides continuing training for our small group (minichurch) leaders.

MINICHURCH LEADER ONGOING TRAINING

Courses: opportunities to sharpen your skills and increase your knowledge	• "Leadership University" • two training workshops per year (only courses that are required) • various seminars on skills such as counseling, conflict resolution, and the like (available throughout the year) • various adult education and discipleship offerings • Center for Church Based Training leadership courses
Community: peers committed to mutual encouragement and accountability	• quarterly "huddles," facilitated by the care pastor, with three to five other minichurch leaders
Mentoring: a relationship that is intentional about your development	• A relationship with a care pastor or coach who is intentional about the minichurch leader's growth and development

Some churches, such as Saddleback Church in Lake Forest, California, are doing a great job of providing online *courses* for their leaders, giving leaders access to training without having to go to more meetings. There is value, though, in at least occasionally gathering leaders together physically, and Fellowship does this twice a year at large training workshops. Each workshop has a central theme, and a number of elective seminars are offered as well. Leadership University is also always available to our minichurch (and other) leaders.

To develop leaders in *community*, the care pastor gathers his or her group of minichurch leaders ("huddle") at least quarterly, typically for a one-night event in someone's home. Once a year, we like to get the huddle group away on a short retreat, so that relationships can build. Huddles have been very effective. Leaders share their own struggles and get perspective from fellow leaders. Leaders learn from each other as they share their successes. We often use a forum format, with the group deciding the agenda and the care pastor facilitating the discussion around that particular topic.

Many leaders develop close enough relationships with the other leaders in their huddle that they relate outside the scheduled meetings. They routinely call each other for advice, prayer, and encouragement. This is especially true when the huddle groups are formed around minichurches that have multiplied into several groups. Often the minichurch leader who multiplied an original group to three or four groups will serve as the care pastor for these new group leaders.

Each minichurch leader has a care pastor as a *mentor*. Often using the *Life Development Planner* mentioned earlier, together they build a simple, customized leadership development plan. One care pastor, for example, is currently working with a minichurch leader in the area of leading Bible discussions. The leader gets nervous when he leads discussions, so he usually delegates the responsibility to another group member. He really wants to learn how to do it himself. Together he and the care pastor have formed a plan: For the next few sessions, he'll meet with the care pastor before each meeting and they'll prepare the discussion together. Then the care pastor will visit the group to observe the discussion and give feedback.

Drawing on this example of equipping small group leaders through courses, community, and mentoring, consider how you could use these dynamics to train various types of leaders in your own church.

CLOSING THOUGHTS

How deep is your team roster? How inspired is your starting lineup? It's easy to get so busy doing ministry that we fail to devote attention to developing others. Yet, the development of people is our real job—even more than accomplishing the tasks.

Bruce: I've begun meeting with a select group of about ten to twelve leaders on a weekly basis for a season of intense development. These are not elders or staff members, but emerging, high-potential lay leaders not currently serving in leadership roles. In the past I thought I was too busy for such a task, but now that I've done this, I've found that the results have been amazing, and I'm persuaded to continue making this a part of my ministry for as long as I'm a senior pastor. I'm considering calling it a "222 group," after God's instruction in 2 Timothy 2:2.

Jeff: Last week Miles shared his story at our church's worship time. Ruben, Miles's coworker and a leader in our church, had invited Miles and his family to church. He came and heard about our discipleship process called *Discovery*. In *Discovery*, he and his wife came to know Christ and began to see their roots grow deeper. Some men in a minichurch began to mentor him in the context of a men's Bible study. He and his wife joined a minichurch and then began to serve in ministry. Now he is in Leadership University and on track to move into leadership in our church. He shared that he couldn't believe how much had happened in his life over the last few years, now leading to an upcoming leadership role in a local church.

As I listened to his story, I was overwhelmed. I realized that *this*—reaching and building into the life of Miles and many, many others just like him—is what the church is all about. If we're not doing this, then what are we doing? As important as our many goals and programs are, we must never lose sight of the reality that developing people always has been and always will be the church's most important job.

To Consider and Discuss

1. What are the main reasons for training emerging church leaders?

2. How is training emerging leaders similar to and yet different from developing existing leaders?

3. How can you build greater "player depth" in your church?

4. What criteria should you use as you construct lists of emerging church leaders? How would you evaluate the entry requirements for "Leadership University" mentioned in this chapter?

5. How could you use the "mentoring, courses, and community" dynamic to develop emerging leaders in your church?

6. What are your next steps, individually and corporately, in the development of emerging leaders in your church?

EQUIPPING YOUR MINISTRY STAFF

10

Any group, large or small, is only as effective as its leadership. If you are responsible for managing a church staff, you are well aware of the importance of your staff firing on all cylinders.

Working with multiple staff presents special challenges in a growing church. What makes a staff person capable at one level of growth won't necessarily carry him or her to the next level. What do you do when a loyal staff member who's helped your church grow isn't equal to the challenge of leadership in what is now a larger church?

A common response is to pressure the staff to work harder. Yet working harder is constrained by physical limitations, and it undermines our need for balanced lives. Plus, working harder seldom produces the desired results.

Another option is to periodically purge your staff of those who fall short of meeting the increasing performance expectations. Though this may occasionally be necessary with people who just aren't wired to work in a large church, this strategy is counterproductive if overused, potentially creating a culture of insecurity, disloyalty, and political maneuvering.

A third option is to invest heavily in staff development and training. Long-term improvement in the quality of church life is dependent on continuing growth in the maturity and ministry skills of the entire church leadership team. Effective development of church staff members must begin with the senior leadership, including the senior pastor, setting the example. None of us ever outgrow the need for ongoing development.

How do we best grow and develop our staff? By now, the answer to this question may be sounding familiar: We need to grow people in knowledge, character, and skills—and we do so through courses, community, and mentoring.

COURSES

It is rare for churches to provide ongoing structured training to equip their staff members or to set aside time for regular staff discussions of key issues that shape the life of the church. *Why would this be?* you may be wondering.

It's a matter of priorities. With the myriad of other demands on church staff members' time, there just doesn't seem to be time for overly busy pastors and staff people to organize, develop, or even attend staff training sessions.

Jeff: When Fellowship began setting aside an hour and a half each week for staff development, we certainly got push-back from the team. How were they going to find the time for this? Occasionally, we still get this reaction, though this response is now rare because we work hard to make sure the time spent adds value to their ministries. In addition to the weekly time, we also schedule occasional retreats and off-site meetings for the same purpose.

Bruce: At McKinney Fellowship Bible Church our pastoral team meets every Monday afternoon. Right now our pattern is to have a staffwide meeting from 1:30 to 2:30 for celebration, information, and affirmation of our vision and values. Then from 2:30 to 5:00 the pastoral team meets for prayer, training, and strategic alignment.

Because prayer has sometimes been difficult for us to prioritize, we make it the first thing we do rather than the last, as we used to do. All too often our prayer times became squeezed out.

We've studied various church-based training courses together, including *Church Leadership* in the Center for Church Based Training's "Leadership Series,"[34] and we have read books together. We value lifelong learning and growing as a team so that we can bind our hearts together as one. Unity is the secret power of the church, often unnoticed until it is disturbed. Unity begins at the leadership level. We want to sharpen each other as iron sharpens iron. At times our interaction is more knowledge oriented, but often it's more devotional and heart related. Occasionally we focus more strategically on specific ministry concerns. It's common for us to challenge each other to keep on running the race— all the way to the end. We don't want anyone on the team to fall out of the race.

BENEFITS OF STAFF COURSES

As a result of our staff discussions—which I'm calling "courses" here—we've seen the following benefits:

Increased Staff Unity

To promote unity, staff members and elders must be of one mind on critical philosophical and theological issues. Spending time discussing these issues—using God's Word as the basis—promotes unity on major organizational, philosophical, and doctrinal matters.

It's easy to make false assumptions about how unified a staff team is—and this is especially true as churches grow. While even church staffs made up of two or three people should be highly intentional about scheduling time for relationship building, the challenge of unity becomes greater as the church grows and the staff increases.

When new staff members are added, long-term staff people can easily assume that the new hires will be fully equipped and pre-pared. More likely, there will be significant gaps in their under-standing of the church's development and ministry philosophy. In our staff discussions at Fellowship, newer staff members have occa-sionally made statements that to the rest of us seem to come out of left field—statements that were inconsistent with our way of doing ministry or seeing the world. The group dynamic can fairly quickly align the person's thinking with the rest of the staff—or at least identify the point of departure. Without the group interac-tion, these new staff members would have continued on a mis-aligned path that may eventually have caused problems.

Our staff discussions also help break down the silo effect com-mon in growing churches—a tendency to develop independent rather than interdependent ministries. Basic alignment is relatively easy with a small staff. You can just go to lunch or have a chat over a Coke. But as the staff grows in size, alignment can break down. A new youth pastor may build a great youth ministry. Then a women's ministry pastor builds a women's department. You hire a few more people. Before long, you have multiple pastors build-ing multiple departments, each operating independently of the others. The church becomes an umbrella for several virtual para-church ministries.

Gaining alignment and building consensus in a silo-dominated culture is almost impossible. The silos must be broken down. Our weekly training time is one element that is helping in this process. Our staff discussions help keep our basic philosophy of ministry, doctrine, values, and strategy at the forefront of people's thinking.

Greater Theological Savvy

Fostering theological reflection within the staff increases staff members' theological sophistication, which enhances their ability to lead their ministries. This is especially true for newer hires who may have come from the business world to a staff where others have a formal theological education. These new staff members may feel insecure in theological discussions because of their relative lack of training. Though they have a lot to offer, they may hold back during important discussions for fear of saying something that is theologically or biblically uninformed.

Over time, taking part in theological reflection with the rest of the staff increases their confidence and their ability to think theologically. At the same time, many of those who come to the church staff from a business environment can sharpen the rest of the staff in such areas as vision, strategy, systems, and change management.

Improved Church Health and Effectiveness

At Fellowship, our staff discussions generate many of our new initiatives. Because we discuss issues apart from the urgency of crises or of forced decisions, our discussions are more proactive than reactive. We evaluate, and then we take action to improve our ministries. Since all the pastors have taken part in the discussions, they have high ownership of the decisions and new initiatives.

GETTING STARTED

How can you make courses a key component of your staff development?

Set Aside a Regular Time to Study and Pray Together

Doing this is a lot harder than it may sound. You will have to powerfully cast the vision for the importance of regular group study and prayer to motivate a busy staff to take time for it. As your discussions generate qualitative change, they will come to see the value of your discussion times—but it takes time. Try for a short-term win. Discuss an issue that you know will generate quick results as a way of building momentum toward establishing a habit of lifelong learning.

At Fellowship, we've found that an hour and a half is about right for our discussions. If we go longer, staff members tend to get nervous about their responsibilities. If we go shorter, the discussions invariably aren't long enough to arrive at implications that translate into action.

Coordinate Your Study with the Governing Board

Ideally, your church staff and board will be covering the same material simultaneously. Our staff and board are too large to be combined for study, but even if they weren't, we would still keep them separate. This separateness allows the elders to evaluate the health of the church and the effectiveness of our staff more freely.

Since Fellowship is elder-led, we place the elder discussions on a timetable just ahead of the staff discussions. This allows the elders to set the tone on values and vision, and the staff can then develop strategies based on the guidance of the elders.

If possible, the same person should facilitate both groups. Doing so can align the two discussions, and each group can benefit from hearing what is happening in the other group. We do, on occasion, combine the two groups, especially if we're leaning toward a major shift of direction as a result of our discussions.

Decide How Much Time to Allocate to Prayer and Training

Being devoted to prayer and the study of God's Word doesn't necessarily require us to spend equal time on each. We do need to be devoted to prayer as a church staff. Decide if you want to include times of prayer in your study times.

Choose the Best Venue for the Sessions

Where you meet shapes the tone of the discussion. Holding your discussions in a home fosters warmth, intimacy, and openness. Holding them at the church office or in a conference room tends to make your discussions more businesslike and action oriented.

Include Emerging Leaders in Staff Discussions

Staff discussions provide a great training and community-building opportunity for your interns and other emerging leaders. Include these folks in these times whenever you can.

COMMUNITY

Probably the single most effective—and least utilized—means of leadership development is the ministry team. As effective as training courses and mentoring can be, they cannot replace the challenge and growth that come from doing ministry together.

Jeff: At Fellowship, the managing pastors decided we wanted to make better use of the development potential of teams throughout the church, and we knew it would have to start with us. So we pastors committed not only to be more intentional about teamwork in our ministry but also to help each other get better. We wanted to be better students of our own strengths, weaknesses, and developmental gaps, as well as better students of each other. We covenanted to speak into each other's lives and opened up our lives to input from the group. We wanted it to be impossible to belong to this ministry team and stay the same.

Although it hasn't always been fun, our commitment to mutual development has revolutionized our individual lives and transformed our team dynamic. Not long ago, an outside facilitator asked, "If any of you on this team were no longer useful to the mission of this church, do you think you would matter anymore to Jeff?" I didn't mind the question, and I was looking forward to hearing the answers. I feel like I'm a pretty nice guy, and I knew that people would say, "Of course! Jeff values everybody. He's such a wonderful leader."

Well, that's not what happened. To a person, the other team members said they believed they would drop off my radar screen completely. They felt that I did a good job signing them up and getting them going but did a lousy job building relationships, communicating value beyond the task, and developing them outside of the context of our ministry goals. While I didn't like hearing that, it rang true. And this revelation led to a broader conversation about all my relationships—including my family—that nailed my tendency to subordinate all my relationships to my sense of mission, which can leave people feeling more like tools than like people.

I'm so thankful my team was willing to challenge me in this area so I could grow. As leaders, we have to be open enough to make such interactions safe—or we'll never enjoy the experience of iron sharpening iron.

Adding mutual development to our team covenant has revolutionized our team in another area as well. In ministry, we typically take our strengths for granted and spend a lot of time trying to compensate for our weaknesses. The typical leader may spend 30 to 40 percent of his or her time in areas of strength and 60 to 70 percent trying to improve, or at least struggle through, the weak areas. Yet that's not how good teams work. So our team covenanted to help each other identify areas of strength and go on to spend 60 to 70 percent of our time working from our strengths. Then we could lean on other team members in the areas of weakness.

Taking this approach has made all of us more productive. I'm a big-picture, visionary kind of person. Some team members are more strategic and systems oriented; others are highly detailed and love to manage implementation. Some of us are better at community building. Our team dynamic has freed me up to do what I love to do and what I'm best at doing—initiating new ideas and recruiting people to form new teams. And it has given others the opportunity to do what they love to do, such as implementing the new ideas and building better strategies and systems than I ever could. For all of us, ministry is far more enjoyable and fruitful. Rather than struggling to get better in our areas of weakness, we are developing our areas of strength.

A staff can exist as nothing more than a roster of people who happen to be at the same level on an organizational chart, reporting to the same person. This, however, is not a team. Ministry teams, with peers challenging and sharpening peers, can be incredibly powerful contexts for leadership development.

MENTORING

For mentoring to be ingrained in the culture of the church, it must begin with the senior pastor. Since other leaders tend to pattern their way of doing ministry after the examples of those who lead them, unless the senior pastor makes mentoring a priority, it never becomes a core value in the church's culture.

For the pastor who supervises other pastors, few responsibilities can claim a higher priority than empowering those they oversee to maximize their potential. This value is especially critical in churches that give preference to a strategy of leadership *development* over one of leadership *acquisition*. Staff development requires time and patience but also has an incredible payoff. While experienced staff members can function quite autonomously, all church staff members need others in their lives who are focused on their continuing growth and lifelong learning.

Bruce: We'll often have one or two staff members who ask for more of my time. I try to meet with them one-on-one. Recently I've been meeting monthly with Mark, an associate pastor in our church who is expressing a desire to plant a church. My student ministries pastor, Paul, asked to meet on a monthly basis for mentoring. When guys ask me, I usually say yes if they're already serving on my pastoral team. I'm looking for those who are straining for more and seeking me out. I asked Mark to email me before our meeting a list of a few crucial issues he wanted to talk about so I could think about them in advance. I can't meet with every staff member each month, but I can invest more deeply in one to three of them.

Without implementing some kind of system with tools for mentoring and holding the mentoring pastor accountable, mentoring won't happen consistently throughout the staff. It's too easy to let other responsibilities crowd it out. Some people are just not natural mentors. Anytime something does not come naturally, we need systems to guide us.

If you are a senior pastor and you want "people developing people" to be valued in your church culture, you must give yourself to developing others around you. You may choose to develop some young emerging leader, but be careful not to do so at the expense of your staff team. Don't expect to see "people developing people" throughout the church's ministries if you aren't showing them how.

CONCLUSION

Building a culture of leadership development in the church must start with the staff and the elders. This doesn't mean, however, that if the staff works at development, it will automatically "trickle down" to everyone else in the congregation. You'll have to be just as intentional about replicating these practices in every ministry throughout the congregation. But it all starts with the core leaders. When the vision of the church as a dynamic leadership incubator is not only talked about by the leaders but also modeled by the leaders, the transformation has begun.

To Consider and Discuss

1. What are some benefits of investing time, money, and energy in staff development? If you are a staff member, why might you want to be involved in a process like this?

2. Which benefits of developing staff are most important to you, and why?

3. How can your church deal with the challenge of limited time for staff development? When could you set aside time for leadership development with your staff?

4. How could "community" and "mentoring" take place in the context of developing your equipping staff members (pastors and ministry directors)?

Equipping
Your Interns

11

Jeff: When I came to Dallas to attend seminary, I had enough ministry experience to realize that the most important decision I would make was which church to serve while I was a student. I wanted to grow through ministry involvement in a local church, and I prayed that God would lead me to a church that took leadership development seriously.

God answered my prayer through a college friend who had just come on staff as a junior high pastor at Fellowship. He asked if I'd be interested in working with him as an intern. I loved the idea of working alongside my friend in ministry and was intrigued by the possibility of being involved in a church that was, by all reports, highly healthy.

Because of previous experiences with unhealthy churches, I came to the internship with great skepticism, just waiting to be disillusioned by the church and its leadership. It looked good from the outside, but I figured that, like pulling the curtain back on the Wizard of Oz, I would soon see it for what it really was. I had read some of the books written by Dr. Gene Getz, the senior pastor, and I respected his thinking, but I figured that the more I got to know him, the more disturbing discoveries I would make. What happened over the next months and years was the exact opposite—and it changed the course of my life.

In time, Bruce Miller, who was directing the leadership development program at Fellowship, invited me to serve as his intern as well, helping him to develop that program. He said, "I want to work with you and train you as if you'll take my job someday. I'm not planning to go anywhere, but I believe you have the potential to be that kind of leader. If you're up for the intensity, put on your seat belt and let's take off!" I jumped into the internship experience with both feet.

During the four years of my internship, I recruited and envisioned teams, counseled troubled people, led a ministry area, taught in various settings, mentored others in ministry, and worked alongside a pastor who initiated some churchwide changes. Because of the breadth of my experience, I learned where I fit and didn't fit on the ministry team. Also during those years various character issues that would never have been noticed in a classroom—such as my tendency to put ministry over marriage and an overuse of charm to manipulate people—were exposed and challenged.

Since I was also a student at Dallas Seminary at the time, my classes took on much greater relevance. I knew what questions to ask, and I was far more motivated to learn. I appreciated the theological and biblical grounding my seminary training gave me, but it alone wouldn't have even come close to equipping me for ministry. It was serving in the context *of* ministry that best equipped me *for* ministry. When I finished my internship, I knew where I fit in ministry. Major character issues had been named and strengthened, and I had received training for the skills I would need for my first professional ministry role.

My internship was the most important developmental experience of my life. God used that time to show me vivid pictures of a healthy church and of strong church leadership. And to my surprise, a few years later I did inherit Bruce's job.

BENEFITS OF INTERNSHIP

Jeff: I am a champion of church-based internships, not only because of how internships have shaped me, but also because I've seen how internships benefit the church. As I've talked with people from other churches that have invested heavily in internships, without exception they share my appreciation for how the internships have strengthened their churches. The many talented and godly men and women who have passed through our internship program have started new ministries, improved existing ones, and provided a "farm team" for new staff hires when we need them. Almost all our current pastoral staff members were developed through our internship process. Having observed them over time, we know what their character is like, what their skills are, and where they best fit in ministry.

Our pastors have also enjoyed the thrill of building into emerging leaders' lives, helping them realize the dream God has planted in their hearts. Over the last fifteen years, we have graduated over two hundred interns. They now serve in ministry literally all over the world. Three years ago, we commissioned four interns and a pastor who was a former intern to plant a church in a neighboring suburb. This past Sunday over fourteen hundred people gathered in that new church to worship God—many of them new converts. Multiplying Christ's church is what church-based internships are all about.

For the interns themselves, the benefits are difficult to overstate. Because we live in a city that has a prominent seminary, about two-thirds of our interns are seminarians. Too often seminary students choose minimal church involvement in order to maximize their academic studies. Upon graduation they realize how completely unprepared they are for their anticipated role. What a contrast to those who have been vitally involved in a highly intentional internship program!

Many of our interns come to us with rough edges. In the internship process, the things that might have crippled their long-term effectiveness are confronted. It scares me to think of all the people who graduate from our seminaries without life-on-life development and who go on to serve in churches. I'm so thankful for a setting in which key character issues can be dealt with in some of our interns—issues that can only be discovered in the context of church ministry.

Other interns come in thinking they have to be the next Chuck Swindoll or Bill Hybels if they're really going to be valuable in the ministry. One former intern, a graduate of both a Bible college and seminary known for producing strong Bible expositors, entered the program completely depressed. He had struggled for over a year to find a ministry position and was convinced that he'd never find a place of significant ministry. He thought valuable ministry could only be expressed through dynamic preaching and powerful visionary leadership. The problem was that he was neither a dynamic preacher nor a visionary leader. In fact, he shared that his every attempt at ministry had failed. Not exactly something you'd want to put on your résumé!

In our first meeting, I drew a tiny box on a notepad and said, "From what you're telling me, this little box is the world of ministry you're trying to squeeze into. The box represents valuable, God-honoring service. But you're having trouble finding success and fulfillment in that box, so you believe you just don't have what it takes to be in ministry." His body language told me I had hit the mark.

Then I started drawing X's over the whole page and said, "What you need to know is that God's kingdom extends far beyond this box. The world of ministry is huge, and you seem to think it's tiny. Christ's mission and your life are both too important to try to squeeze into a box where you don't belong. If you're meant to be here, or over here, or way over here, then you owe it to yourself and God's kingdom to spend your life serving the way God intended. Quit looking for a job. Spend the next year or two as an intern, and let us help you find who you really are and what it means to express God's dream for your life."

It didn't take long to find out that he was wonderfully gifted for ministry, that he was compassionate, creative, and relationally strong. He began to flourish in hands-on social outreach, meeting the tangible needs of people in our community. He is now thriving in a ministry that fits him to a tee.

IS SEMINARY ENOUGH?

Jeff: Imagine that you are about to have open-heart surgery. Your very young doctor introduces himself, explains that he has never done open-heart surgery before (you get to be the first!), but assures you that you are in good hands because he has passed all his cardiology classes. Would you be comforted?

Fortunately, this isn't how things happen in medicine. Doctors don't simply read some books, take some tests, then start performing surgery. My brother is a cardiologist. After completing medical school, he spent another five years doing internships, residencies, and fellowships. Doctors are intensively trained to practice medicine in the context of practicing medicine.

Why, then, would we train pastors, whose job is to tend to matters of the spirit, any differently? Does it make any sense to assume that a person is ready for pastoral ministry just because he or she has completed a theology degree? Doesn't it make a lot more sense to equip people *for* ministry in the context *of* ministry? Certainly Bible college or seminary training is valuable, but as a supplement to church-based training, not as a substitute for it.

STARTING AN INTERNSHIP PROGRAM

How do you start an internship program? What are the characteristics of an effective internship ministry?

CHOOSE INTERNS WHO ARE A GOOD FIT WITH YOUR CHURCH

Interns who come from within your own congregation probably already fit. They've grown up with your ministry philosophy and forms. In time, a successful internship program will attract people from other churches and cities to your church—especially if your city contains a seminary or Bible college.

When someone we don't know calls to inquire about our intern program, we reply, "We're happy you're interested. Why don't you get involved in the church, volunteer to participate in ministry, and in a few months we'll talk about a possible internship? You first need to know if Fellowship is really the church for you." This introductory period also gives us the opportunity to observe the prospect in ministry to see if he or she is qualified.

SEEK LONG-TERM COMMITMENTS TO THE PROGRAM

Long-term internships allow you to more accurately identify people's strengths and weaknesses and to observe improvement over time. Internships of just a few weeks or months do not allow enough time for significant development in areas of character, skill, or relational ability.

A few years ago, we became aware of a problematic lifestyle issue in one of our interns—an issue we never would have identified in a short internship. As a result, we were able to provide a counseling and development plan with the intent of reintroducing him to the internship program a year later. He came back into the program a changed person. In a short-term internship, the issues wouldn't have surfaced.

We believe one year of service as an intern is minimal. A two- to four-year commitment is ideal. In internships lasting more than two years, consider adding a residency level. In a residency, a person who has been an intern for more than two years can move to a greater level of responsibility. In our model, the intern moves from managing projects within a ministry area to leading a ministry area. This transition from internship to residency provides a natural evaluation point to confirm if the individual should continue on a path to professional ministry.

ASSIGN INCREASING LEVELS OF RESPONSIBILITY

Too often internships involve only menial tasks rather than significant ministry opportunities. Since pastors shouldn't simply do ministry for people, but rather equip others—including their interns—to do ministry, it is their privilege to give away significant responsibility and provide encouragement and feedback to the intern. Over time, if the intern is faithful, his or her responsibility should grow.

We expect our interns to take risks and to be willing to fail. We tell them, "Your internship experience is the one time in your life where someone else will take the blame if you fail, but you get the credit if you succeed. Enjoy it while you can!"

You will have to guard the value of doing ministry through developing others, because internships can quickly deteriorate into a means whereby pastors get cheap help. If you work with interns or are charged with leading an internship program, you will have to be the champion for interns being involved in genuine, frontline ministry.

PROVIDE IN-DEPTH MINISTRY EXPERIENCE

It's important for the intern to focus his or her ministry in one area (children's ministry, for example) for an extended period of time (a year, for example). Doing so allows growth over time and gives the intern an opportunity to learn an area of ministry well. Interns who bounce from one area to another too quickly gain ministry exposure but not in-depth development.

The ministry area itself also receives maximum benefit when an intern invests a longer period of time. Plus, the intern develops deeper relationships and gets to see what a ministry area is like in various seasons of ministry over the course of a year or years.

PROVIDE A BROAD EXPOSURE TO MINISTRY

Make sure you give interns opportunities to see more than just their own ministry areas. At Fellowship, we have a mandatory intern meeting every other Monday evening where various pastors share a "live issue" from their ministry with the group. We have chosen a case study approach to most of the meetings, allowing for discussion around real issues rather than just listening to a presentation. We try to share current crises with the intern crew before the crises are resolved and the lessons too neat and tidy.

As an intern, I learned a great deal from a difficult experience. One of our pastors was discovered to be having an affair. Throughout the whole process of unraveling the details and deciding just how to deal with all the people and complications involved, our senior pastor, Gene, regularly gave updates to us interns. He invited us to the meeting at his home where the two people—in separate sessions—confessed to the staff team. I saw Gene and the elders show incredible wisdom and grace through a devastating time in the life of the church. I learned more from that experience than a hundred classes could teach. Had Gene not had a vision for our development as interns, we wouldn't have had access to the inner workings of the process. I'll be forever thankful that he shared the vision we are describing.

Find ways for interns to broaden their ministry exposure beyond your own local church as well. You may want to develop partnerships with area churches that are different enough from yours to expand your interns' view of ministry. We regularly invite other area pastors to share in our meetings. We'll occasionally take field trips to observe other ministries in action.

A few years ago, we worked with a highly creative pastor in San Francisco to design an "urban plunge" in the inner city. I asked the pastor to design experiences that would make us completely uncomfortable. I didn't want to do even one thing that we could do in suburban Dallas. We stayed in a shelter that was being renovated. We worked with teen runaways, homeless people, and those dying from AIDS. We ministered alongside non-Christians in secular organizations as well as in inner-city churches. That trip changed each of us forever and gave us a picture of ministry in a setting quite different from ours.

MAKE MENTORING A HIGH PRIORITY FOR PASTORS

The quality of the internship experience hinges to a large extent on the relationship between pastor and intern. Maintaining a high level of quality in pastoral mentoring often feels like an uphill battle. However busy they may be, pastors must be held accountable for their intentionality in developing interns.

Don't assume that your pastor (or pastors) already knows how to mentor. Getting good results requires constant envisioning and training. Additionally, you will need to develop reporting procedures to get regular feedback from both the pastor and the intern on their progress. The old axiom "You can't expect what you don't inspect" surely holds true when you are trying to hold busy pastors accountable for developing interns in addition to carrying out their other responsibilities.

Set realistic expectations regarding the mutual responsibilities of both pastors and interns. We ask the pastor to work with his or her intern to draw up a development plan. This plan includes identifying the intern's dreams for future ministry and the current gaps in their knowledge, character, and ministry skills that may keep these dreams from becoming a reality. They can then plan how to close these developmental gaps and measure progress.

GIVE REGULAR FEEDBACK

Evaluation is critical to the internship process. Our pastors provide monthly feedback, and twice a year they conduct a more extensive review to discuss progress in character, knowledge, and skill development. Yet, any time an intern performs a ministry task, you're wasting a key opportunity if you don't provide immediate feedback.

A friend once shared a tip about giving feedback that has helped tremendously. Include quickly in your feedback these two words: "Next time." For example, you might say, "You did a great job. Next time you teach, add a little more energy, and it will even be better." By doing this, you're affirming that there is a "next time." It's much better than saying, "Boy, when you taught you should've had a lot more energy. It really dragged."

INCLUDE BIBLICAL AND THEOLOGICAL TRAINING

A trend among some churches that develop leaders through internships is to downplay the importance of theological education. As a result there are churches that develop interns in practical skills and send people off to minister who may have proven leadership skills but limited theological depth. If this trend continues, it will be very damaging to the church. More than ever, we need leaders today who are astute theologically, who have a good grasp of church history, and who have comprehensive biblical knowledge and understanding.

We insist that interns pursue theological education along with their more practical ministry experience. Since we live in a seminary town, many of our interns receive theological training through the seminary. For some of our interns, we use church-based theological education materials developed by groups such as the Center for Church Based Training, BEE International, and BILD International. Most seminaries also provide distance learning options so that any church can have access to theological education, regardless of location.

COMPENSATE INTERNS WHEN POSSIBLE

Paying interns for their work frees them up to focus on their ministry and personal development. They are able to invest more time in learning and serving.

In a recent discussion with several pastors who run intern programs, the topic of pay came up. One pastor seemed proud that his church did not pay its interns, and he gave multiple reasons for the policy. Another pastor responded to him by saying, "Then why don't you make the same commitment as a pastor? All the same reasons apply." After that response, paying people who are involved in ministry didn't seem like such a bad idea after all!

At Fellowship, we currently have eleven paid interns/residents and about eight volunteer interns. When a paid position opens up, we give our volunteers consideration for the opportunity. No one except the intern director and the mentoring pastor know which interns are paid and which are not. We keep this confidential to avoid creating two status levels in the program. We learned this the hard way. Early on we didn't do this, and some viewed the paid interns as the "real" ones and the volunteers as something less. We hold both paid and unpaid interns accountable, yet we are more flexible in our expectations with volunteers regarding the number of hours they work. We allow them to decide how many hours a week they can work, and then we hold them to their decision.

SUPPORT INTERNS IN THE PLACEMENT PROCESS

Fewer churches these days seem to be looking to seminary placement offices to fill positions. They either hire from within their own ranks or they network with churches they know and respect to identify potential candidates. If you have an effective internship program, it's likely that word will get out to other churches that will contact you about their staffing needs. As this begins to happen, it is important to have a system in place to channel these requests to your interns. Be ready to give objective evaluations of interns to those who contact you. Be up-front with your interns about your recommendations. You may also want to develop a networking process yourself to uncover ministry opportunities for the interns you are developing.

Bruce: I traveled to New Zealand in the early 1990s to conduct a board retreat for Church Based Training New Zealand (CBTNZ) and to speak at a conference. On my last day in Auckland Brad and Rochelle Carr invited me to have dinner with them in their apartment. Brad told me of his desire to go to seminary in America. At the time I was the director of the internship program at Fellowship. I talked with him about our program. It wasn't long after our conversation that Brad came to study in Dallas and became an intern at Fellowship. In 1996 when Fellowship sent me out to plant a church in McKinney, Brad asked if he could join the team. Fellowship graciously agreed to continue Brad's intern salary and to send him with me.

In those initial years, Brad served in nearly every capacity. Not only did I have him join us on the advisory team (our top leadership team before we appointed elders), he was also a full member of the pastoral staff. Brad was involved in everything from setting up chairs to helping lead our first capital campaign. In addition, I met with Brad regularly in a mentoring capacity.

Knowing that it involved risks, I began entrusting Brad with an increasing window into the inner workings of the whole church and staff. This involved bringing Brad into confidential matters regarding how I viewed and dealt with staff conflicts or inadequacies—sensitive issues about those who were at that time his peers. I tried to help Brad see and feel through me what it would be like one day when he became a senior pastor of a church plant.

Knowing that Brad wanted to plant a church in Auckland, McKinney Fellowship Bible Church began setting aside funds for this effort, unknown to Brad. A few years later, after serving for a season as co-pastor of Auckland Bible Church (ABC), Brad formally unveiled the plans for a church plant from ABC, and we presented him with a significant gift to be used in launching the church. We intend to partner with him, helping to pay his salary for the first two years to provide a catalyst for launching our first international church plant.

CONCLUSION

An internship program can be a highly effective way to grow your church and expand God's kingdom. We (Jeff and Bruce) are certainly thankful for a church that chose to invest in our lives and set us on a course for a lifetime of ministry. And we're grateful to God when we think of over two hundred people serving all over the world who were developed through our internship program. Your church will benefit greatly and God's kingdom will grow as you make it a priority to develop future leaders through church-based internships.

To Consider and Discuss

1. Why would a church consider developing an internship program?

2. What principles are important to consider in building a vital internship?

3. How do you see courses, community, and mentoring functioning with interns?

4. How should "heads," "hearts," and "hands" be addressed in an internship program?

5. How could you envision your church starting an internship program? What would have to happen to prepare the way?

EPILOGUE: THE FUTURE OF CHURCH-BASED TRAINING

What could happen in your church if you fully embraced church-based training? Can you imagine what might be happening ten years from now? How does the following scenario sound?

Every ministry in your church flourishes, with quality leaders bearing fruit for Christ. Leaders are initiating new ministries in the community that show and tell the love of Jesus. Jail ministries, latchkey kids afternoon outreaches, 5-kilometer runs for the homeless shelter, and recovery groups of every kind have emerged. Your local community is looking to your church for leadership in dealing with crime, the low-cost housing shortage, and racial issues, as well as teen pregnancy and school dropout problems.

In fact, your church has developed so many quality leaders that you don't have room for them all, and you are exporting them to other churches and needy areas around the world. A new global vision team has drafted a plan to plant new churches in countries all over the world, with leaders developed in your own church. Leaders who grew up in your church and cut their leadership teeth in your ministries, leaders your people love and respect, are now being called by God to plant churches with teams sent out from your church. The excitement and passion for Christ's mission have never been higher.

Dozens of your church's leaders are rising up to go on mission projects, both short-term and long-term. Some are able to support themselves financially or to be tentmakers in foreign countries. As they come back and tell their stories of God's work through them, the vision-fires for developing leaders burn even hotter. Your church's impact for Christ is increasing beyond the wildest dreams of your founding families.

Because the leaders have spent so much time praying together and studying God's Word, your team exhibits exceptional unity and maturity. Your board and staff members experience a depth of relational connection and spiritual life that is opening up huge ministry in many lives. Spiritual transformation is commonplace. The average person extends the leadership challenge regularly to other average people, who are stepping up to make a difference for God.

PARTNERSHIPS WITH OTHER CHURCHES

What if your church wasn't alone in this effort, but many other churches also accepted the challenge and responsibility to raise up leaders? What could God do in your community, in your city, in your society? Local churches helping other local churches in dynamic win-win partnerships reflects the New Testament pattern (Jerusalem and Antioch, for instance) and moves Christ's kingdom work forward.

We envision growing numbers of churches creating their own resources and courses for their own settings, thus becoming teaching churches. What a blessing to the kingdom if many churches were to begin producing resources they could share with other churches! The church of Jesus Christ needs more resources on more topics; churches need different kinds of resources for different situations. So many culturally specific issues need addressing. Resources need to be translated into other languages and adapted for different cultures.

Bruce: In traveling to Nigeria with Musa Asake, the general secretary of the Evangelical Church of West Africa (ECWA), I saw firsthand and heard the huge need to develop church leaders in Third-World countries.

PARTNERSHIPS WITH TRAINING INSTITUTIONS AND ORGANIZATIONS

Partnerships can extend from local churches to other kingdom organizations such as schools, mission agencies, parachurch groups, and associations of churches. Whole denominations and networks of local churches could embrace a new way of training leaders. They could begin movements where local churches could reclaim their central role in the training of Christian leaders.

Christian colleges, Bible colleges, and seminaries provide the kinds of learning opportunities few local churches can offer. We dream of effective partnerships between local churches and Christian schools at both the undergraduate and graduate levels. What Tim Dearborn, associate director for faith and development at World Vision International, said rings true: "As in business, the future of theological education rests in creative partnerships between multiple institutions that enter into joint ventures in order to design and deliver a better 'product' than could be done autonomously."[35] How wonderful it can be for local churches and seminaries to bring their respective strengths to the table and work together to develop leaders for Christ's church!

Promising first steps have been taken to establish church-seminary partnerships that we believe point to the prospect of even more effective synergistic approaches. Too often churches have become merely locations for school extensions. As we look to the future, we can envision local churches becoming full partners so that the strengths of church-based training and traditional theological training are brought together in the lives of those preparing for ministry.

Parachurch groups such as Campus Crusade for Christ, The Navigators, and Young Life could partner with local churches in developing opportunities for church-based training. Equipping organizations such as T-Net International, Sonlife Ministries, Church Resource Ministries, and teaching church networks could work with churches to develop church-based training strategies.

A PROPOSAL

In discussions of church-based training, often the first question asked is, "Could this be an alternative to going to seminary?" The answer is yes. We are not, however, opposed to seminary, nor do we see church-based training programs as a necessarily better route for a person who wants to enter professional ministry. At the same time, with the increasing cost of schooling, with more people making halftime shifts from business to ministry, and with the maturing of church-based training models, more individuals, churches, and groups are coming to regard church-based training as a fully viable training path for professional ministry. This reality compels those who are involved in church-based training to develop full-fledged programs for those needing a professional level of training.

Emerging leaders who look to church-based training as their primary preparation path for professional ministry often raise the next logical question: What kind of credentials can be offered? The issues of assessment, accreditation, and recognition are complex and difficult.

We offer a proposal for future consideration. Rather than making institutional accreditation or academic degree programs the basis for church-based training credentialing, we suggest that the church-based leadership development movement look to postgraduate professional and trade certifications as a model for recognition. Some of these are globally recognized, which is an important factor for a church leader in our shrinking global village.

Post-graduate certifications can carry far more weight than degrees. For instance, a BA in accounting is nice, but it can't compare with a CPA. Lawyers who have degrees but who haven't passed the bar cannot practice law. Numerous professions and trades recognize proficiency through designations such as "board certified" in medical fields, and "certified financial planner" or "life underwriter" in the finance and insurance industries. In the trades, you can earn certifications as an auto mechanic generally and for specific brands (Mercedes, Volvo) that are recognized anywhere cars are driven in the world.

We are suggesting the creation of a post-graduate recognition by local churches that would carry far greater weight than a degree from a Bible college or seminary. This certification would require extensive practical experience, in addition to rigorous training, perhaps the passing of an exam, and character and competency recommendations. (If you're interested in seeing a more fully developed draft copy of this proposal, visit the Center for Church Based Training's website at www.ccbt.org.)

You can count on this: The globalization of theological education will change the face of the church. Most Bible colleges and seminaries are in the West and most trained Christian leaders minister in Western cultures. Yet, the need for trained leaders in Africa, Latin America, and Asia is huge. Already more Christians live outside Western countries than inside them. The church in the developing world is crying out for leadership development resources and systems. While the church is exploding with new converts in some parts of the world, when these converts don't get sufficient training, they're lapsing into heresy or syncretism. The global church desperately needs church-based training. Even in the West, Austria doesn't have a single evangelical Bible college or seminary. Nigeria has thousands of pastors who have received only the most minimal training. Thankfully, organizations such as TOPIC (Trainers of Pastors International Coalition) are emerging to address this need, but much more must be done.

We dream of global partnerships between and among churches in different countries. Imagine churches that possess resources promoting the vision of helping local churches all over the world develop leaders in their churches. Your church can help meet this crucial global need for Christ's church. Include leadership development in your missions vision and budget. Get involved in the translation, production, and distribution of training resources. Step out and personally help develop leaders. The leadership development needs of the churches in China alone are so great that it would take thousands of churches to begin to address them.

What is God doing with church-based training? His ways are far beyond ours, but to us it looks as though he is up to something big. A global renewal appears to be afoot, and it has something to do with church-based leadership development. God is calling his churches back to their mandate to develop leaders (Ephesians 4; 2 Timothy 2:2). For Christ's mission to flourish and his church to multiply all over the world, local churches must pick up the baton of leadership development. As individuals we need to be passing batons to the leaders we develop. As churches, we need to be passing batons to other churches.

God has given you a baton. What will you do with it?

To Consider and Discuss

1. What do you dream would happen through your church if you were to really take church-based leadership development seriously?

2. What other churches can you partner with in this effort both locally and globally?

3. Are there other organizations you could partner with to develop leaders in your church?

4. How do issues of accreditation and recognition affect the people of your church?

5. How can your church play a role in the glaring need to develop leaders for Christ's church around the world?

6. What do you think God may be up to with the growing movement of church-based training?

APPENDIX 1:
THE SIX-STEP WISDOM PROCESS: A LEARNING ENGINE FOR LIFE

BRUCE MILLER

As a student at the University of Texas in Austin, I enrolled in Plan II, the university's liberal arts honors program, where I experienced an interdisciplinary approach to education. The experience prepared me for seminary, where I majored in systematic theology. A few years later I would come back and teach theology, specializing in theological "prolegomena" (introduction to theology) with a focus on theological method.

To earn income during seminary, I ran a tutoring business that required me to interact with all kinds of learning styles. After seminary I pursued doctoral work in "the history of ideas" at the University of Texas in Dallas and was involved with a church-based ministry called BILD International. Through these experiences and my own research, I was exposed to each of the following fields— all of which have helped to shape what we've come to call the Six-Step Wisdom Process (chapter 4), a learning approach many hands have helped refine.

ADULT LEARNING

Recently specialists in learning theory have discovered differences between the way children learn and the way adults learn. While pedagogy has studied how children learn, a newer field called "andragogy" researches how adults learn. Rarely do adults sit down and read a thick manual to learn everything about how a new DVD player works; rather, they usually pick up the manual when there's a problem to solve. More precisely, adults read the specific section they need in order to fix whatever is broken or to accomplish a task, such as recording from one disc to another.

Since adults are often unmotivated to learn facts in a vacuum, a skillful teacher will create a context for learning. The late Paulo Freire, a world-famous Brazilian educator, argued for a problem-posing approach to teaching adults. When confronted with a problem to solve or an issue to address—especially if something important is at stake—most adults are highly motivated to find a solution. For instance, a Christian who ordinarily has little interest in in-depth Bible study may become motivated to research what Scripture says about marriage and divorce when facing the possibility of a divorce.

In the local church the stakes are high. We are dealing with people's lives. We had better get it right. Before leaders will be motivated to study a topic, they typically need to understand the problem that needs to be addressed. We are much more motivated when we have a clear *need to know*, so a good educational approach with adults will "problematize" the issues and help learners see what is at stake.

WORLD MODELS OF ADVANCED LEARNING

At some of the finest and oldest schools around the world, we find the issue-driven approach to learning at the highest levels. Harvard Business School uses case studies in which students must read about a particular complex issue in the real world and offer their plans for addressing the issues involved. At Oxford and Cambridge universities, students are assigned to tutors who guide them through readings by using penetrating questions. In doctoral seminars around the world, professors meet weekly with their top students to discuss common readings. The professor doesn't lecture but facilitates a discussion with probing questions about the reading they have studied. When we face our most intractable political and social struggles, we look to think tanks composed of the brightest and the best. These small groups of brilliant people work together on how best to understand and address global economic, social, and ethical problems.

POSTMODERNISM

In the kind of advanced learning that takes place in these world models, the participants are aware that the answers to most questions are not black-and-white. For all of its mixed baggage of good and bad, postmodernism appropriately highlights ambiguity and the impossibility of simple, straightforward, always-correct solutions to most of life's questions.

Modernism came at life through logic. Math and science were considered the carriers of the cleanest, clearest thinking. We assumed that to each human problem there existed a neat answer like a geometric proof; if we just thought harder and got more data, then we would find "The Answer." The twenty-first century has shined the spotlight on the limitations of modernity. Most of life is messy. Most of the issues involved in raising children well or in deciding how to allocate a church budget do not have simple answers. These are not fill-in-the-blank questions for which there are answers in the back of the book. Rarely can major life issues be resolved simply by acquiring more knowledge (although more information is sometimes needed). Sorting out how to live life well and how to lead Christ's church well demands wisdom. Younger people, who more fully embrace a postmodern mentality, by and large prefer to learn through dialogue and discussion rather than through lecture. Why? Because they're not after facts that can be read on the Internet, copied into charts, and displayed on Power-Point. They are after wisdom.

ANCIENT INSIGHTS

This postmodern insight into the complexity of reality and the need for more than knowledge is not new. The leading thinker and educator in fifth-century BC Greece was Plato, the great student of Socrates. Since Socrates didn't write any books, it was Plato who gave us the Socratic method. In his dialogues Plato teased out truth and wisdom by having several characters discuss an issue in a way that gave birth to fresh insights and showed the limitations of shallow solutions. Plato believed the best leaders would be those who loved wisdom—literally philo-sophers (lovers of wisdom). By asking excellent questions Plato hoped to guide his students into truth and draw out from them deeper wisdom than they were conscious of at the start of the conversation. Today we talk about the synergy that comes from a team. Research into creative and critical thinking shows that a team will almost always come up with more and better ideas than just one individual. Today, in a world in search of better answers, the Socratic method is regaining popularity.

Plato's student Aristotle built on his teacher's ideas and created many of his own. Most of Western philosophy looks back to Plato and Aristotle as the greatest influences on all who have followed them. In his ethical theory, Aristotle identified a sense he called *phronesis.* Having wrestled with what it means to make good choices and live a virtuous life, Aristotle realized that it involved much more than simply following the rules, and even more than applying general principles to individual circumstances. How to live a virtuous life couldn't be contained in an axiom or even a set of principles; it required *phronesis,* the ability to exercise practical, ethical judgment. A person with *phronesis* knows which principles to apply in each particular situation and learns from making choices in each unique circumstance so as to improve future judgments. For instance, when is courage foolishness? When do you show mercy and when do you enforce justice? The church today needs wise leaders who can exercise *phronesis.* The church needs to be asking, "What kind of educational design will help nurture *phronesis?*"

THEOLOGICAL METHOD

In modernity, theology was understood to be the memorization of truths. It was a catechetical approach: Learn "The Answers to The Questions." All the answers were given in the creed or confession. Nonconfessional traditions often viewed the answers in just as black-and-white a way. However, theology today is becoming a verb. More than simply describing a set of truths, theology describes an activity: We *do* theology. To theologize is to think biblically and comprehensively about an issue. We stand, to be sure, on the two-thousand-year-old foundation of Christian theologizing, but out of that solid, orthodox core faith, many matters need continual intense, penetrating thought in terms of what they mean for us today in our faith communities. Ancient truths need fresh expression and internalization for each generation.

Good theology is not only solidly founded on God's Word; it is also actively developed in the context of the church. It is ecclesial as well as biblical. The best theology is done in community with other believers, pursuing Christ's mission to advance God's kingdom. Systematic theology draws on the resources of the Word primarily, but also on Christian tradition, culture, and experience. The best leaders for Christ's church should be able to do theology.

BIBLICAL PATTERNS

When Moses instructed Israelite parents, he told them to teach their children about God's Word and God's ways (Deuteronomy 6). For their future survival in the midst of pagan nations, Israel needed to pass on the faith. On a practical level, the next generation needed to know what God had done for their forefathers and who he was in contrast to the gods of the religions around them. They needed to be able to do theology for their day.

How did their parents pass on the faith? They were to teach God's Word in the course of life as they walked down the road and as they put their children to bed. Truth and wisdom were conveyed in the midst of life as it happened. Today, in the course of church life, we need to be passing on the faith to the next generation, teaching our emerging leaders how to think biblically about all matters of life. This pattern of teaching is depicted again in the Old Testament Wisdom literature, where sayings, proverbs, and analogies provoke us to think about how God views life.

Jesus models a similar educational design. As he and his disciples traveled through Judea, Jesus commented on the things they saw and the events that happened. He asked penetrating questions and challenged his disciples to reflect on what others were saying. He would begin, "You have heard that it was said . . . " and "What do you think . . . ?"[36] As the master teacher, Jesus led his disciples to understand the kingdom of God and their role in it. Rarely did he lecture, especially to his closest disciples; most often he engaged in dialogue.

Like Jesus, we need to engage in developing the emerging leaders around us. I suggest we consider using a similar approach to Jesus' approach—one that draws from the best research in adult learning theory and the finest in ancient classical education, one that works well in our postmodern world. In evaluating various materials and resources for developing leaders, we should pay attention to educational design. Ideally it would be great to come up with a design informed by Old Testament models that taught people how to do theology, how to exercise practical biblical wisdom in real life.

The Six-Step Wisdom Process attempts to do just that, combining time-honored learning methods with a solid approach to doing theology. The courses produced by the Center for Church Based Training use this process to cultivate biblical wisdom so that future church leaders will be prepared for the complex issues they will face. Our hope and prayer is that repeated use of these six steps will teach people to think theologically in a way that produces biblically wise actions.

APPENDIX 2: ASSESSING THE WHOLE PERSON: AN INVENTORY FOR CHURCH LEADERS

ROWLAND FORMAN

Use this inventory to identify gaps in your knowledge of God and his Word, your character, and your ministry skills. It is designed to give you a snapshot of your development—not to discourage you. Here are some ways to get the most out of this inventory:

Knowledge
- Complete the knowledge part of the inventory on your own, making notes of next steps you want to take.
- Meet with a mentor to discuss your next steps and build in some accountability.

Character
- Complete the character part of the inventory.
- Give a copy of the character section to a friend and ask him or her to complete an assessment of you.
- Meet with your friend and compare your friend's scores with your own.

Skills
- Complete the ministry skills section.
- Meet with a mentor or your leadership team to discuss next steps you will take to develop new ministry skills.

KNOWLEDGE: WHAT DO YOU KNOW?

Knowing the Word

	Never Read	Read Parts	Read All	Studied In-depth	Taught
Genesis	☐	☐	☐	☐	☐
Exodus	☐	☐	☐	☐	☐
Leviticus	☐	☐	☐	☐	☐
Numbers	☐	☐	☐	☐	☐
Deuteronomy	☐	☐	☐	☐	☐
Joshua	☐	☐	☐	☐	☐
Judges	☐	☐	☐	☐	☐
Ruth	☐	☐	☐	☐	☐
1 & 2 Samuel	☐	☐	☐	☐	☐
1 & 2 Kings	☐	☐	☐	☐	☐
1 & 2 Chronicles	☐	☐	☐	☐	☐
Ezra	☐	☐	☐	☐	☐
Nehemiah	☐	☐	☐	☐	☐
Esther	☐	☐	☐	☐	☐
Job	☐	☐	☐	☐	☐
Psalms	☐	☐	☐	☐	☐
Proverbs	☐	☐	☐	☐	☐
Ecclesiastes	☐	☐	☐	☐	☐
Song of Songs	☐	☐	☐	☐	☐
Isaiah	☐	☐	☐	☐	☐
Jeremiah	☐	☐	☐	☐	☐
Lamentations	☐	☐	☐	☐	☐

	Never Read	Read Parts	Read All	Studied In-depth	Taught
Ezekiel	☐	☐	☐	☐	☐
Daniel	☐	☐	☐	☐	☐
Hosea	☐	☐	☐	☐	☐
Joel	☐	☐	☐	☐	☐
Amos	☐	☐	☐	☐	☐
Obadiah	☐	☐	☐	☐	☐
Jonah	☐	☐	☐	☐	☐
Micah	☐	☐	☐	☐	☐
Nahum	☐	☐	☐	☐	☐
Habakkuk	☐	☐	☐	☐	☐
Zephaniah	☐	☐	☐	☐	☐
Haggai	☐	☐	☐	☐	☐
Zechariah	☐	☐	☐	☐	☐
Malachi	☐	☐	☐	☐	☐
Matthew	☐	☐	☐	☐	☐
Mark	☐	☐	☐	☐	☐
Luke	☐	☐	☐	☐	☐
John	☐	☐	☐	☐	☐
Acts	☐	☐	☐	☐	☐
Romans	☐	☐	☐	☐	☐
1 Corinthians	☐	☐	☐	☐	☐
2 Corinthians	☐	☐	☐	☐	☐
Galatians	☐	☐	☐	☐	☐
Ephesians	☐	☐	☐	☐	☐
Philippians	☐	☐	☐	☐	☐
Colossians	☐	☐	☐	☐	☐

	Never Read	Read Parts	Read All	Studied In-depth	Taught
1 Thessalonians	☐	☐	☐	☐	☐
2 Thessalonians	☐	☐	☐	☐	☐
1 Timothy	☐	☐	☐	☐	☐
2 Timothy	☐	☐	☐	☐	☐
Titus	☐	☐	☐	☐	☐
Philemon	☐	☐	☐	☐	☐
Hebrews	☐	☐	☐	☐	☐
James	☐	☐	☐	☐	☐
1 Peter	☐	☐	☐	☐	☐
2 Peter	☐	☐	☐	☐	☐
1, 2, & 3 John	☐	☐	☐	☐	☐
Jude	☐	☐	☐	☐	☐
Revelation	☐	☐	☐	☐	☐

Summary

Which books of the Bible do you plan to study next? When?

Knowing Bible Doctrine

How would you rate your knowledge of the following Bible doctrines (based on your ability to explain each doctrine adequately to a new Christian):

	Inadequate				Adequate
God's Attributes	1	2	3	4	5
The Trinity	1	2	3	4	5
God the Father	1	2	3	4	5
God the Son	1	2	3	4	5
God the Holy Spirit	1	2	3	4	5
Scripture	1	2	3	4	5
Humanity	1	2	3	4	5
Salvation	1	2	3	4	5
Sanctification	1	2	3	4	5
Angels	1	2	3	4	5
Satan	1	2	3	4	5
The Future	1	2	3	4	5

Summary

Which Bible doctrines do you plan to study next? When?

CHARACTER: WHAT ARE YOU LIKE?

The following are twenty characteristics of maturity in Christ, taken from Paul's letters to Timothy and Titus. The categories have been adapted from *The Measure of a Man* by Gene Getz. Also included are nine aspects of the fruit of the Spirit from Galatians 5:22–23.

The five-point scale asks you to rate yourself from "inadequate" to "adequate."

Qualities of a Church Leader Inventory: Personal Assessment

	Inadequate				Adequate
1. Overall Spiritual Maturity—Your overall maturity as a Christian	1	2	3	4	5
2a. Above Reproach—Your reputation as a Christian among fellow believers	1	2	3	4	5
2b. Above Reproach—Your reputation among non-Christians	1	2	3	4	5
3. Marital Faithfulness—Your relationship with your spouse	1	2	3	4	5
4. Temperate—The degree to which you maintain balance in your Christian experience	1	2	3	4	5
5. Prudent—Your ability to be wise and discerning	1	2	3	4	5
6. Respectable—The way your life reflects the life of Jesus Christ	1	2	3	4	5
7. Hospitable—Your kind and generous spirit	1	2	3	4	5
8. Able to Teach—Your ability to communicate God's truth clearly (whether in a group or one-on-one)	1	2	3	4	5
9. Not Addicted to Wine—Your ability to control various obsessions and compulsions	1	2	3	4	5
10. Not Self-Willed—Your ability to relate to others without being self-centered and controlling	1	2	3	4	5
11. Not Quick-Tempered—Your ability to control your anger	1	2	3	4	5

	Inadequate			Adequate	
12. Not Pugnacious—Your ability to control any form of verbal or physical abuse	1	2	3	4	5
13. Gentle—Your ability to be objective and fair-minded in your relationships	1	2	3	4	5
14. Uncontentious—Your ability to avoid arguments	1	2	3	4	5
15. Free from the Love of Money—Your ability to be nonmaterialistic	1	2	3	4	5
16. One Who Manages His/Her Own Household Well—Your ability to function in your family role according to God's plan	1	2	3	4	5
17. Loving What Is Good—Your ability to "overcome evil with good"	1	2	3	4	5
18. Just—Your ability to be just and fair in your relationships with others	1	2	3	4	5
19. Devout—The way your life reflects God's holiness	1	2	3	4	5
20. Disciplined—Your ability to live a disciplined Christian life	1	2	3	4	5

Fruit of the Spirit Inventory:
Personal Assessment

	Inadequate			Adequate	
1. Love—Your ability to love others unconditionally	1	2	3	4	5
2. Joy—Your ability to be happy and joyful despite your circumstances	1	2	3	4	5
3. Peace—Your ability to be calm under pressure	1	2	3	4	5
4. Patience—Your ability to persist when circumstances or people disappoint you	1	2	3	4	5
5. Kindness—Your ability to be generous and kind	1	2	3	4	5
6. Goodness—Your ability to do what is morally and ethically right	1	2	3	4	5
7. Faithfulness—Your ability to be depended on	1	2	3	4	5
8. Gentleness—Your ability to treat people with tenderness	1	2	3	4	5
9. Self-Control—Your ability to be self-controlled and not controlled by circumstances	1	2	3	4	5

Summary

Discrepancies between my assessment and that of my friend:

from the Qualities of a Church Leader Inventory

_____

_____

_____

_____

_____

_____

from the Fruit of the Spirit Inventory

_____

_____

_____

_____

_____

_____

Character qualities I need to work on in this next period:

from the Qualities of a Church Leader Inventory

_____

_____

_____

_____

_____

_____

from the Fruit of the Spirit Inventory

_____

_____

_____

_____

_____

_____

MINISTRY SKILLS:
WHAT CAN YOU DO?

Ministry Skills Inventory

Please complete the categories that apply to your ministry situation.

Administration	Inadequate			Adequate	
1. Your organizational skills	1	2	3	4	5
2. Your ability to delegate	1	2	3	4	5
3. Your ability to manage time	1	2	3	4	5
4. Your ability to communicate clearly with the people you lead	1	2	3	4	5
5. Your ability to think and plan strategically	1	2	3	4	5

Leading

6. Your ability to cast vision of a preferred future for the group you are leading	1	2	3	4	5
7. Your ability to set goals for a group of people	1	2	3	4	5
8. Your ability to equip other people for ministry rather than doing it all by yourself	1	2	3	4	5
9. Your ability to lead a small group	1	2	3	4	5
10. Your ability to lead an entire church	1	2	3	4	5
11. Your ability to lead worship in your church	1	2	3	4	5

Shepherding

12. Your ability to counsel needy people	1	2	3	4	5
13. Your ability to correct false doctrine	1	2	3	4	5
14. Your ability to encourage people who are in special need	1	2	3	4	5
15. Your ability to mentor emerging leaders	1	2	3	4	5
16. Your ability to resolve conflict in your ministry team	1	2	3	4	5

	Inadequate				Adequate
17. Your ability to teach the word of God in a church setting	1	2	3	4	5
18. Your ability to conduct a wedding	1	2	3	4	5
19. Your ability to conduct a funeral	1	2	3	4	5

Disciple-making

20. Your ability to evangelize unbelievers	1	2	3	4	5
21. Your ability to make close friendships with unbelievers	1	2	3	4	5
22. Your ability to nurture new believers	1	2	3	4	5
23. Your ability to conduct a baptism	1	2	3	4	5
24. Your ability to conduct the Lord's Supper	1	2	3	4	5
25. Your ability to facilitate a group discussion	1	2	3	4	5

Other Ministry Skills

List any other ministry skills you would like to develop in the future:

_____

_____

_____

_____

_____

_____

Summary

From the Ministry Skills Inventory (and any other skills you have listed), which skills would you like to develop in the next period?

_____

_____

_____

_____

_____

_____

_____

Notes

1. Seeing the need for developing leaders in the revival of Christianity in the early 1980s in Vienna, Willi Giefing began doing church-based training. Early informal efforts among the young churches later culminated in BAO (Biblische Ausbildung am Ort [Biblical Training on Location]), a ministry that was focused on German-speaking Europe and now reaches into Croatia and other countries. BAO (www.bao.at) has offices in Austria, Germany, and Switzerland.
2. See, for example, David Hesselgrave, *Planting Churches Cross-Culturally: A Guide for Home and Foreign Missions* (Grand Rapids: Baker, 1980), 52–63.
3. Clairvoyance (Self-Portrait) 1936 oil on canvas by René Magritte, Galerie Isy Brachot, Brussels, Belgium. Copyright © 2003 C. Herscovici, Brussels/Artists Rights Society (ARS), New York. Used by permission.
4. Edward Farley, *Fragility of Knowledge: Theological Education in the Church and the University* (Philadelphia: Fortress, 1988), 86.
5. Stephen R. Covey, *The Seven Habits of Highly Effective People* (New York: Simon and Schuster, 1989), 97.
6. See John Adair, *Effective Strategic Leadership* (London: Pan Books, 2002), 7.
7. See Bill Thrall, Bruce McNicol, and Ken McElrath, *The Ascent of a Leader* (San Francisco: Jossey-Bass, 1999), 8.
8. Robert Greenleaf, *Servant Leadership* (Mahwah, N.J.: Paulist Press, 1983), 7.
9. Samples can be ordered at www.ccbt.org.
10. Cited in Kent and Barbara Hughes, *Common Sense Parenting* (Wheaton, Ill.: Tyndale House, 1995), 3.
11. Hughes, *Common Sense Parenting.*
12. Wayne Cordeiro, *Doing Church as a Team* (Ventura, Calif.: Regal, 2001), 205.
13. Stanley J. Grenz, *Created for Community* (Grand Rapids: Baker, 1996), 51.
14. Grenz, *Created for Community,* 216.
15. Robert E. Coleman, "The Lifestyle of the Great Commission," in D. A. Carson, ed., *Telling the Truth* (Grand Rapids: Zondervan, 2000), 259.

16. See Günter Krallmann, *Mentoring for Mission* (Hong Kong: Jensco, 1994), 55.
17. Cordeiro, *Doing Church as a Team*, 204–5.
18. Charles M. Olsen, *Transforming Church Boards into Communities of Spiritual Leaders* (Bethesda, Md.: Alban Institute, 1995), 25–26.
19. Reggie McNeal, *A Work of Heart* (San Francisco: Jossey-Bass, 2000), 132.
20. See Jeff Jones and Rowland Forman, *Life Development Planner* (Dallas, Tex.: Center for Church Based Training, 2002).
21. J. Robert Clinton, *The Making of a Leader* (Colorado Springs: NavPress, 1988).
22. See Ted W. Engstrom, *The Fine Art of Mentoring* (Brentwood, Tenn.: Wolgemuth and Hyatt, 1989), ix.
23. Fred Smith, "Spotting a New Leader," *Leadership* 17 (Fall 1996): 4:31–33.
24. Paul D. Stanley and J. Robert Clinton, *Connecting: The Mentoring Relationships You Need to Succeed* (Colorado Springs: NavPress, 1992), 43.
25. Ruth Barton, "How to Grow a Leader," *Discipleship Journal* 92 (March/April 1996), 67.
26. Carl George, *Nine Keys to Effective Small Group Leadership* (Mansfield, Pa.: Kingdom, 1997), 19, 61.
27. The original "Skunk Works" refers to a division of Lockheed Martin that gained fame for their inventions that pushed the limits of aviation technology. The term has come to refer to a group of people who, in order to achieve unusual results, work on a project in a way that is outside the usual rules. A "Skunk Works" is sometimes used to spearhead a product design that thereafter will be developed according to the usual process.
28. See Larry W. Osborne, *The Unity Factor: Developing a Healthy Church Leadership Team* (Vista, Calif.: Owl's Nest, 1989), 80.
29. See Exodus 12:1–20; Numbers 9:1–14; Esther 9:18–32; Luke 22:7–30; 1 Corinthians 11:23–25; Revelation 3:20; 19:9.
30. See Gene A. Getz, *The Measure of a Man* (Ventura, Calif.: Gospel Light, 1997).
31. George, *Nine Keys to Effective Small Group Leadership*, 54–55.
32. Print materials for *Discovery* are available through the Center for Church Based Training (www.ccbt.org); order by telephone at 1-888-422-2896.
33. Bill Thrall, Bruce McNicol, and Ken McElrath, *The Ascent of a Leader* (San Francisco: Jossey-Bass, 1999); Donald S. Whitney, *Spiritual Disciplines for the Christian Life* (Colorado Springs: NavPress, 1997); Tom Clegg and Warren Bird, *Lost in America* (Loveland, Colo.: Group, 2001).
34. For more information, log on to www.ccbt.org.
35. Tim Dearborn, "Preparing Leaders for the Church of the Future," *Frontiers: Evangelical Perspective on Faith and Society* (Spring 1996).
36. See, for example, Matthew 5:21, 27, 31, 33, 38, 43; 17:25; 18:12; 21:28; 22:42.

Subject Index

Center for Church Based Training:
www.ccbt.org

At the heart of church-based training is a conviction on the part of local church leaders for
the spiritual training of every person entrusted
to their care, as well as to provide opportunities
to develop those who desire to serve in ministry
leadership roles.

The Center for Church Based Training assists local church leaders
in the development of such a training process, an intentional pathway
of growth built around their vision and values. To aid in the process,
CCBT offers training opportunities and resources designed specifically around church-based ministry initiatives.

Training Opportunities

Annual Conference

Church-based training is not simply another program to try in your
church. It is a value, a process of developing people, that permeates
every ministry in your church. At the annual conference you and your
leadership team will hear from practitioners who have implemented
church-based initiatives in their own local churches. You will also
have the opportunity to select from a variety of elective workshops
designed for specific ministry training.

Regional Workshops

CCBT workshops are held throughout the United States and are
designed with individual tracks that will

- provide an introduction to church-based training processes
  and principles;
- assist leaders in taking next steps in their church-based
  ministry plans; and
- lead governing board members through a process of
  understanding their roles and responsibilities.

Church-Based Resources

The Discovery Series (also available in Spanish)

This series is designed to help participants understand foundational truths of the Christian faith, be confident of what they believe, and develop a biblical worldview so they begin to think biblically about the issues of life.

The Life Development Planner

Understand how your background has been purposely arranged by God to make you the person you are. Isolate developmental gaps in your biblical knowledge, ministry skills, and character, and then design a plan to close the gap. Ultimately, you will develop a life development plan to provide direction and perspective for you and your ministry.

The Leadership Series

This series will help leadership teams work through the role of a New Testament church and the responsibilities of those who lead it. You will also form both a biblical theology and local strategy for the mission of your church. The series is designed to train and unify existing leadership teams and to develop emerging leaders.

The Elders and Leaders Field Guide

The task of shepherding men and women in the church is complex and demanding, requiring that leaders deepen their knowledge of God and his Word, develop godly character, and hone their ministry skills. This guide has been developed to lead governing board members through a "learning in community" process that will result in renewed unity, vision, and purpose.

The Center for Church Based Training
1700 Gateway Boulevard
Richardson, TX 75080
972-997-4410; toll-free: 1-888-422-2896
www.ccbt.org

We'd love to continue the conversation with you. Contact us at *LeadershipBaton@ccbt.org* with your feedback, questions, and insights.

We want to hear from you. Please send your comments about this book to us in care of zreview@zondervan.com. Thank you.

ZONDERVAN.com/
AUTHORTRACKER
follow your favorite authors